Knit-pearls for you

This book contains 50 fun patterns from the grassroots of Icelandic knitting and crocheting.

Twenty knitters from all over Iceland provided us with original designs, and we carefully selected those projects we found most interesting and exciting. The result is a mix of the knitters all-time favorite patterns, designs they've developed and honed over many years or even projects that have a special sentimental value for them. There are even a few that were designed especially for this book.

The projects vary from small to large and are suitable for knitters and crocheters at all skill levels, from the very experienced to those just taking their first steps crafting.

Icelandic knitters tend to use Icelandic wool for most of their projects, and so many of the patterns in the book specify Icelandic wool as the yarn to use. We hope that you'll get a chance to use Icelandic wool for at least some of your projects, but if not, you can of course substitute it for other kinds of yarn. Just make sure that you use a yarn that gives you the gauge specified in the pattern.

In Icelandic, the book is called *Prjónaperlur – prjónað frá grasrótinni*, which, when directly translated, means Knit-pearls – knits from the grassroots. The book's title refers to the contributing knitters and their patterns, all of them so beautiful, delightful and unique, like the finest pearls.

We hope that the book's patterns and knitter's introductions will cheer and inspire you to tackle new projects and to keep on knitting and knitting... and knitting... And of course crocheting too!

Enjoy a life full of knits!
Erla and Halldóra

Visit our blog at *www.icelandknits.com*

Our favorite pancake recipe

A note to friends and relatives of knitters:

First of all: You are not alone. There are many more like you out there. People who feel left out and ignored at home and prioritized somewhere way behind the yarn. We just want to tell you that what you see as a problem (all that knitting!) is really a source of joy, creativity and energy (you just haven´t realized it yet.) Why don´t you rather play along and make these fabulous pancakes and some good coffee for your knitter? Believe us, by doing so, you'll finally get some attention. And we're sure it will make both of you happy.

1 1/3 cup flour
1/2 teaspoon baking soda
1-2 tablespoon sugar
1/4 teaspoon salt
1-2 eggs
1 2/3 - 2 cups of milk
25 g butter, melted, or 2 tablespoons vegetable oil
1 teaspoon vanilla essence

Mix all ingredients together, apart from the butter. Melt it, and let cool a little before mixing it together with the rest. Ladle a thin layer of batter onto a pan and fry both sides of the pancake.

These are typical Icelandic pancakes. They should be wafer-thin and are best enjoyed sprinkled with sugar or covered with jam and whipped cream. The recipe is enough for about 12-13 pancakes.

Enjoy!

Víglundur has got the hang of it

Efnisyfirlit

HATS

MITTENS

SWEATERS

SOCKS

SHAWLS AND SCARVES

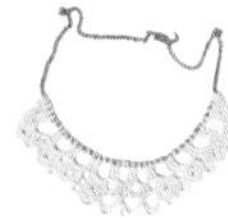

JEWLERY

SKIRT

CUDDLE ANIMALS

OTHER

READING

Eva Rós

Eva Rós Ólafsdóttir is a 25 year old social work student from Hafnarfjörður in South-West Iceland. She's the mother of an 18 month old boy who you could say is the source of her knitting obsession. Eva Rós is already a dedicated knitter and designer even though she only took up knitting a year ago! She'd tried to knit before when she made three honest attempts at a scarf, but didn´t find it a particularly exciting project. It wasn't until last year that she discovered the magic of top-down knitting and became hooked on the craft. She's had help with her knitting from her mother and her grandmother, as well as from other moms, who she met while on maternity leave and refers to as "ridiculously good knitters." While on leave, they met up once a week with the babies and their knitting, and still meet regularly and inspire each other. Eva soon started to knit „outside the box" without using patterns, as she finds it difficult to follow a pattern without changing it. Eva Rós is a self-proclaimed hyperactive knitter who uses every spare minute to knit, and so can be found knitting at school, on the bus, when a passenger in a car or sitting in front of the TV. Even her young son has already learned how to avoid getting tangled up in his mother's yarn! Check out Eva's knitting activities at www.handahlaup.wordpress.com.

Knitting motto: *Frog if you have to – it will only make your finished piece better in the end!*

Monkey Cardigan

- knit top-down

"I wanted to knit a top-down Lopi sweater, and I wanted it to be different from the traditional Icelandic Lopi sweaters. My son is really interested in all kinds of animals, but sweaters with duck, cat and dog patterns have already been designed. I therefore chose monkeys for this sweater, as they also fit perfectly to my "different" theme."

This sweater is knit top-down. Start with the neck, and then divide the stitches between the sleeves and front and back pieces. When the yoke is completed, the sleeve stitches are placed on a stitch holder or scrap yarn while you finish the body. The advantages with knitting a top-down sweater is that you can try the sweater on any time while knitting it, so you can adjust the sleeves accurately to the length of the arms. And you can also easily add length to the sleeves later, as the child grows, by undoing the cast-off at the cuff of the sleeves and adding a few rows.

Size: 1.5-2 (4) years. Chest circumference: 64 (68) cm/25 (27) inches, length from the neck down: 40 (43) cm/15½ (17) inches. Sleeve length: 22 (24) cm/8½ (9½) inches.
Yarn: Lopi lite or another yarn of a similar weight in dark brown (250 g), light brown (50 g), light green (50 g), white (50 g). Lopi lite is a worsted/light worsted yarn, and has approx. 100 m (109 yd)/50 g.
Needles: 3.5 and 4.5 mm (US 4 and 7) circular needles, 40 and 60 cm/16 and 24 inches long, as well as double pointed needles.
Other: 4 stitch markers, 6 buttons, and a sewing machine.
Gauge: 18 stitches and 24 rows in stockinette stitch on 4.5 mm needles make 10x10 cm/4x4 inches. Adjust needle size if necessary to obtain the correct gauge.
Abbreviations: KFB: knit in front and back of the same stitch.

Cast on 58 (62) stitches for the neck on 40 cm/15½ inches circular needles. Two stitches are purled down the whole sweater's front; they mark where the sweater will be steeked and cut to be made into a cardigan and are therefore not counted in the total number of stitches from now on. Join to knit in the round, and work 1x1 rib (knit 1, purl 1) for 8 cm/3 inches. Now change to 4.5 mm (US 7) needles, knit stockinette stitch, and divide the sweater into back, front and sleeves, like this: *row 1:* purl the 2 stitches in the middle of the front piece. Knit 9 (10) stitches across the left front, increase by knitting both in front and back of the next stitch (KFB), place marker, KFB again, knit 6 stitches across the sleeve, KFB, place marker, KFB, knit 18 (20) stitches across the back, KFB, place marker, KFB, knit 6 stitches across the other sleeve, KFB, place marker, KFB, knit 9 (10) stitches across the right front piece. *Row 2:* knit (but don't forget to purl the two stitches in the middle front). *Row 3:* purl the two stitches in the middle of the front piece, and then: [knit to the last stitch before the marker, KFB, move/slip the marker to right needle, KFB], repeat around. Repeat row 2 and 3 until the sleeve stitches are a total of 46 (48), and the back 58 (62) stitches and each front piece 29 (31), a total of 208 (220) stitches. **Divide for sleeves and body:** purl the 2 middle stitches, knit to next marker, place the 46 (48) sleeve stitches on a scrap yarn. Knit the 58 (62) back stitches, place the 46 (48) sleeve stitches on a scrap yarn, knit the remaining 29 (31) stitches. Now work only on the body 116 (124) stitches, the sleeves are knit later. Knit 4 (6) rows, increase 4 (3) stitches evenly spaced in the first row = 120 (128) stitches. Now knit the **treebranch pattern** from the chart. Knit 4 (6) rows, then knit the **monkey pattern** from the chart. Since the sweater is knit top-down you start to knit the pattern in the upper left corner of the chart. Knit until the body measures 18 (21) cm/7 (8½) inches from sleeve opening. Then switch to 3.5 mm (US 4) needles and knit 1x1 ribbing (knit 1, purl 1) for 4 cm. Bind off.

Arnar Kári happy with his monkeys

Read all about how to use stitch markers on page 24.

Eva Rós

Sleeve: place the sleeve stitches on 4.5 mm (US 7) needles. Pick up 1 stitch under the arm = 48 (50) stitches. Knit 4 (6) rows. Decrease 0 (2) stitches under the arm. Now knit the **treebranch pattern.** After that, decrease 2 stitches under the arm, and again in every 6th row for a total of 7 (6) times = a total of 34 (36) stitches. Knit until the sleeve measures 18 (20) cm/7 (8) inches from the underarm. Change to 3.5 mm (US 4) needles and knit 1x1 ribbing for 4 cm/1½ inches. Bind off. Knit the other sleeve. Cut the sweater open, like this: using a sewing machine, sew two seams with small stitches in each of the purled stitches up the front of the sweater, four seams in all. Carefully cut to open the sweater between the two purled stitches. **Buttonband:** pick up stitches for the buttonbands; pick up a stitch for every row along the steeks, stitches are then decreased in first row. *Row 1:* [knit 1, purl 1, knit 2 together, purl 1, knit 1, purl 2 together], repeat until end of row. *Row 2-4:* knit 1x1 ribbing. *Row 5:* bind off. **Buttonholes** are made on one of the buttonbands in row 3 by knitting 2 together, yarn over. The top and bottom buttonholes are made 1 cm from the upper/lower edge, and the other 4 evenly spread there inbetween. **Finishing:** weave in all ends. Fold the neckline down and fasten. Sew the buttons on.

Perla

There are 264 monkey species in the world and here we've added one more. This one is surely one of the cutest species of monkey - and it´s knittable!

Treebranch pattern

Start here to knit the treebranch pattern on the sweater

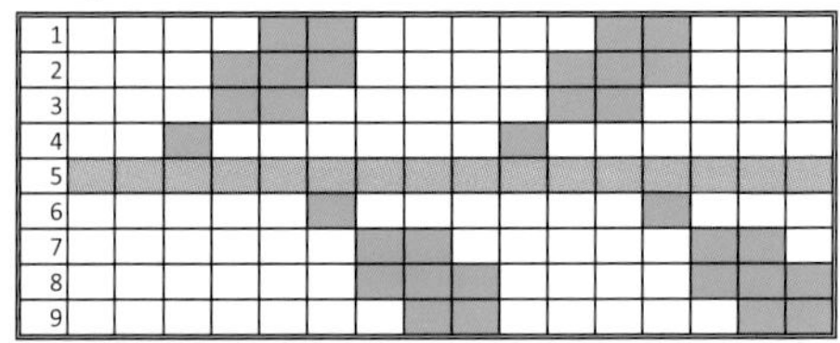

Start here to knit the treebranch pattern on the hat

Just look at these cute little monkeys! We didn´t want to turn them upside-down in the book... It is however better to do so when you knit them because this sweater is knit from the top down.

Monkey pattern

Start here to knit the monkey pattern

x: skip stitches in smaller size

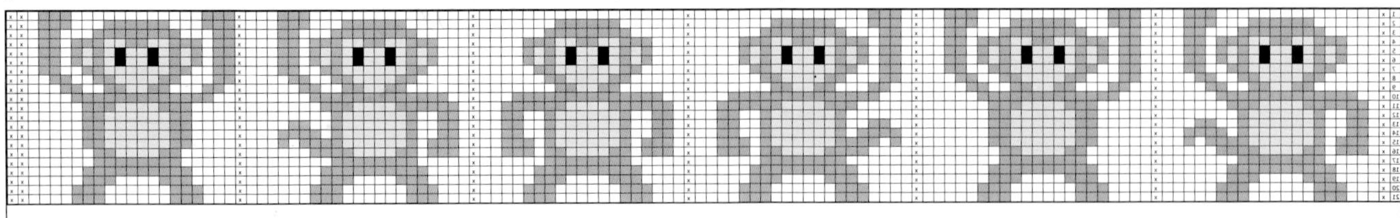

Matching Monkey Hat

Size: 2-4 years.
Yarn: Lopi lite or another yarn of a similar weight, same colors as in the sweater: Dark brown (100 g), light brown (50 g), light green (50 g). Lopi lite is a worsted/light worsted yarn, and has approx. 100 m (109 yd)/50 g.
Needles: 3.5 and 4.5 mm (US 4 and 7) circular needles, 40 cm/16 inches long as well as 4 mm (US 7) double pointed needles.
Gauge: 18 stitches and 24 rows in stockinette stitch on 4.5 mm (US 7) needles make 10x10 cm/4x4 inches.

Cast on 80 stitches with dark brown yarn on 3.5 mm (US 4) circular needles. Join to knit in the round and work 1x1 ribbing (knit 1, purl 1) for 10 cm/4 inches. Change to 4.5 mm (US 7) needles and knit stockinette stich, 8 rows. Now knit the treebranch pattern from the chart. Knit until the hat measures 11-13 cm/ 4½ – 5 inches from the rib, then start the decreases. Change to double pointed needles when the stitches become too few to fit on the circular needles. **Decreases:** Row 1: [knit 8 stitches, knit 2 together], repeat until end of row. Row 2: knit. Row 3: [knit 7 stitches, knit 2 together], repeat until end of row. Row 4: knit. Repeat thes two rows with decreasing number of stitches between the decreases until only 8 stitches are left. Break yarn and pull through the remaining stitches. Weave in all ends. Fold the rib and fasten loosely with a needle and thread.

Jóhann & Guðný

Jóhann Jóhannsson and Guðný E. Kristjánsdóttir from Stöðvarfjörður in the East of Iceland are both in their early 60s and knitting as happily as ever. Guðný has always been an avid knitter, and never sits down without a project to work on. Jóhann had an accident that kept him from work for a while, so he took up knitting to pass the time. He had originally learned to knit as a child, and luckily he had his wife to help him to get going again. Jóhann now believes that knitting saved his sanity while he was unable to work. He started to knit mittens to sell decorated with a special Nordic star pattern he found among one of his late mother's old knitting patterns, and it didn't take him long to put his own twist on the pattern. The star on this ear-warmer is the original one, though. In the evenings the couple sits, each in their own Lazy Boy chair, knitting together. At a regional get-together held several years ago, Jóhann and Guðný performed a little sketch about themselves. They played themselves, sitting side by side in their Lazy Boy chairs, knitting as the phone rang. The phone kept ringing and ringing and neither of them got up to answer because they were both too busy with their knitting. They are seriously considering getting themselves headsets for the telephone so they won't lose precious knitting time when answering calls!

Knitting motto: *Knitting makes you patient*

Ear-warmer from the East

"We have knit this ear-warmer with all kinds of color patterns, but the Nordic star, as seen on this particular ear-warmer is always a favorite. The headband has picots on the edges, which some might find a bit feminine, so for men who want to knit or use these it's very simple to just skip the picots. We encourage you to play around with the colors in the pattern."

Size: adult size medium.
Yarn: Icelandic unspun wool, 2 strands held together, or other yarn of similar weight that gives you the same gauge. The Icelandic unspun has approx. 300 m (328 yd)/100 g.
White and dark gray, 50 g of each – but any contrasting colors work well for this ear-warmer.
Needles: 5.5 mm (US 9) circular needles, 40 cm/16 inches long. Adjust needle size if necessary to obtain the correct gauge.
Gauge: 15 stitches in stockinette stitch with the yarn and needles reccommended should be 10 cm/4 inches.

Cast on 80 stitches, loosely. Join to knit in the round and knit 9 rows. Then knit the picot edge, or knit 1 purled round if you prefer to skip the picots. The picots are knit like a row of eyelets, like this: [knit 2 together, yarn over], repeat until end of row. When the ear-warmer is folded on the eyelet row, the picots become visible. Knit 2 rows. Now knit the pattern as shown in the chart. After that, knit 3 rows, and then knit a picot row like before: [knit 2 together, yarn over], repeat until end of row – or purl 1 row to omit the picots. Knit 10 rows (only 9 rows are visible from the picot row) and bind off loosely. Fold the edges in along the picot row or the purled row and use a darning needle and some yarn to fasten the edges to the wrongside of the ear-warmer. Wash in luke warm water and lay to dry.

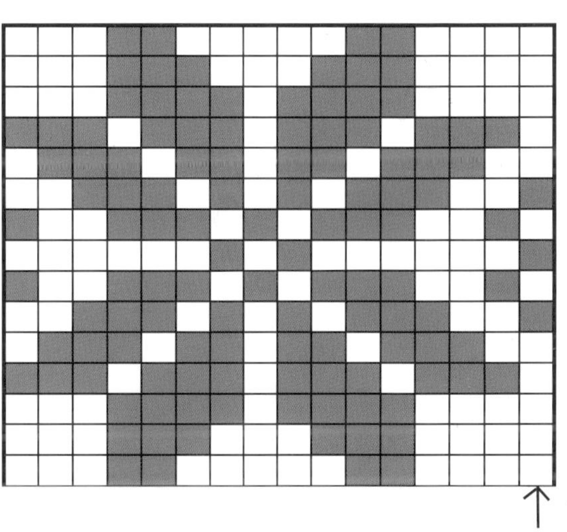

Hrönn

Hrönn Konráðsdóttir is a 29 year old multitalented and energetic archaeologist from Reykjavík who excavates old, Icelandic artefacts. She is a passionate knitter, as well as a flamenco dancer in her spare time (no, not with her knitting needles). She has knit since an early age but her interest in knitting increased a lot when studying handicraft at the Breiðholt junior college, so she now always has something on her needles. She knits a lot to give away, especially for the children of friends and family: „Knitting always calls for more knitting, people are always asking for something knitted, and you get entangled in the knitting". Her boyfriend also benefits from her knitting obsession and is the regular and happy recipient of handcrafted hats, socks and sweaters. Check out Hrönn´s knitting activities at www.hronnkonn.blogspot.com

Knitting motto: *One stitch at a time*

Magical Mittens

Hrönn´s magical mittens are both gloves and mittens. She designed them for use when excavating, as archaeologists need to be able to work outdoors, and write and draw without their fingers constantly freezing. The magic symbol on the back of the hand, knit with intarsia, is very old. These mittens are quite magical –try them for yourself!

Size: medium.
Yarn: Lopi lite, 100 g for the main color (brown or black), and 50 g white for the pattern. Lopi lite has approx. 100 m (109 yd)/50 g.
Needles: 3.5 and 4 mm (US 4 and 6) double pointed needles, and a 3 mm (US C) crochet hook. Adjust needle size if necessary to obtain the correct gauge.
Gauge: 19 stitches and 26 rows make 10x10 cm/4x4 inches.
Other: 2 small buttons.

Right mitten: Cast on 40 stitches on 3.5 mm (US 4) needles (it's a good idea to use 2 needles held together when casting on, for the cast on to be loose). Divide the stitches evenly between 4 needles. Join to work in the round, and knit 2x2 rib (knit 2, purl 2) for a total of 16 rounds. Now switch to 4 mm (US 6) needles and knit stockinette stitch. Knit 18 rows, on the next row make the opening for the thumb: knit the first 2 stitches on needle 1, then knit the next 5 stitches on to scrap yarn for the thumb opening. Move the five scrap yarn stitches back on to the left needle and knit them again with the main color. Knit to end of row. Knit 13 rows, or up to the fingers, each finger is now knit separately. **Fingers:** divide the stitches so you have 5 stitches on the first needle, 15 stitches on needle 2, 15 stitches on needle 3, and 5 stitches on needle 4. Now knit the first finger (the indexfinger): knit the 5 stitches on needle 1, cast on 2 stitches with the backward-loop cast on, then knit the 5 stitches of needle 4 = 12 stitches. Divide the stitches evenly between 3 needles, and join to knit in the round. Knit 14 rows, bind of loosely. Put the next 5 stitches on a needle, and put 5 stitches from the other side on a second needle (for the middle finger). Pick up 1 stitch on each side of the finger = 12 stitches. Similarily, divide the stitches evenly between 3 needles to knit this finger in the round. Knit 16 rows, then bind off loosely. Knit the next finger (the ring finger) in the same manner, except knit 14 rows instead of 16. The last 10 stitches are for the last finger (the little finger), pick up 1 stitch on each side of that finger as well = 12 stitches. Knit 12 rows, cast off loosely. **Top of mitten:** cast on 20 stitches with 3.5 mm (US 4) needles, do not join in the round. Knit 1x1 ribbing back and forth for 3 rows. Now pick up 20 stitches with 4 mm (US 6) needles on the back of the hand, two rows below where the fingers start. Join these 20 stitches with your 20 stitches on the 3.5 mm (US 4) needles – let them lie in the palm of the hand. Join to work in the round and knit 2 rows with 4 mm (US 6) needles. Knit the Magic symbol from the chart on the back of the hand with white yarn. Since there is no pattern in the palm of the hand, pull the white yarn back behind the magic symbol to be worked in the next pattern row, but be careful not to pull to tigthly.

Decreases for the top of the mitten: start side decreases during the last row of the magic symbol pattern. Decrease row: needle 1: knit 1 stitch, slip 1, knit 1, pass the slipped stitch over the knit one, knit to end of needle. Needle 2: knit until 3 stitches are left on the needle, knit 2 together, knit 1. Needle 3: same as needle 1. Needle 4: same as needle 2. Knit 1 row. Now knit the decrease row for every row until 8 stitches are left. Break yarn, leaving a long tail (you will later use the tail to crochet a small button-loop), and pull through the remaining stitches. **Thumb:** remove the scrap yarn to pick up the thumb stitches. Pick up 10 stitches and divide evenly between 3 needles. Also pick up 2 stitches on each side of the thumb = 14 stitches. Knit 9 rows. Now cast off 4 stitches in the middle of that side of the thumb that faces the palm to make a little opening. Cast on 4 stitches in the next row right above the four stitches that you just bound off. Knit 2 rows, then decrease stitches on the sides of the thumb like you decreased on the sides of the mitten, decreasing 4 stitches/row for the next two rows, omitting the plain knit row in between decrease rows, and leaving 6 stitches. Break yarn, pull through the remaining stitches.

Left mitten: Same as the right mitten, except the thumb is placed on needle 2. When it is time to make the thumb opening (on the 19th row from the ribbing), knit needle 1. Needle 2: knit until 7 stitches are left on the needle, knit 5 stitches on to scrap yarn, move these 5 stitches back to left needle and knit them again with the main color and then knit the remaining two stitches on the needle. The fingers are knit just like the fingers on right mitten, except the order of the fingers is reversed so that the first finger (the indexfinger on the right mitten) is now the little finger, and thus only 12 rows, the next one (the ringfinger) is 14 rows, the middle finger is 16 rows, and the indexfinger is 14 rows. **Finishing:** weave in all ends, except the one on the top of the mitten. Sew a button on to the ribbing, in the middle of the back of the wrist, to fasten the top of the mitten when the fingers are exposed. Use a 3 mm (US C) crochet needle and and chain 6 with the yarn on top of the mitten to make a buttonhole for the button. Single crochet to fasten the loop near the base of the loop. Weave in the end.

Abrakadabra... the mittens are ready!

Magic symbol pattern

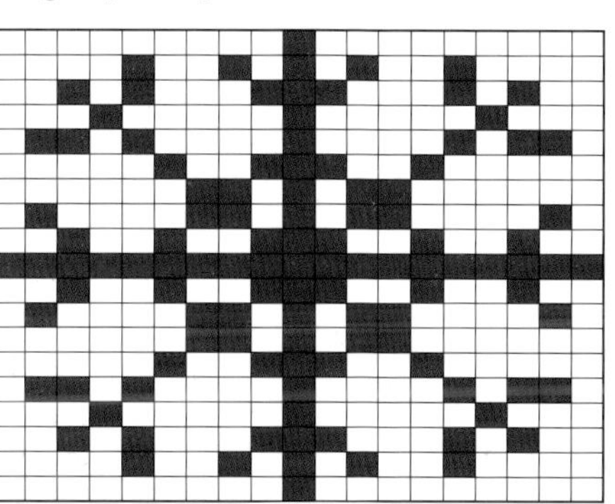

Decreases for the sides starts here

Start here to knit the pattern

Ingibjörg

Ingibjörg Ólafsdóttir is a 51 year old fashion designer, tailor –and, of course, knitting master. She teaches textile arts and fashion design in Garðabær junior college just outside Reykjavik, and through her job she gets to express some of her creativity. Not all of it though, as she always has many knitting and sewing projects going on at home as well. Ingibjörg began her knitting career at the age of 8 when her mother taught her how to knit. She herself has taught her three daughters to knit and says they've all become very good at it – not surprising considering they've had such a good teacher! In recent years, Ingibjörg's grandchildren have started to arrive, and she loves to knit for them. She's mainly knitted colourful mittens for them so far. Ingibjörg sometimes uses knitting patterns, but prefers to improvise. She especially loves lace knitting and uses lace patterns in many of the things she makes. She also likes to mix materials, like combining hand knitting and sewn fabric in one and the same piece. She says her choice of yarn dictates what she´ll make, and that she, for example, will make a totally different sweater from red yarn than from green yarn!

Knitting motto: *Start with something small and then add to it*

Mittens knit with sock yarn

If you knit Einband or other laceweight yarn together with the sock yarn you get bigger mittens

Preschool Mittens

"I have repeatedly knit these mittens for my 4 year old grandson ever since he was 2 years old. He lives in Stockholm and is always so happy when his mother gives him the mittens to wear on his way to preschool in the colder months. On those occasions, he often says: „Oh, are these the mittens my granny made for ME?" The mittens form a special connection between us, since we live so far apart. I sometimes make them in pink, which is a color he loves. The mittens are lightweight and supple for little hands, perfect for a child who likes to pick up interesting stones and other treasures on the way home from preschool. You can make the same pattern knitting Einband (Icelandic laceweight) together with the sock yarn and using bigger needles for slightly bigger mittens."

Size: 2-3 (3-4) years. If you knit Einband or other laceweight yarn together with the sock yarn in the 3-4 year old size you get bigger and thicker mittens that would fit a 5-6 year old.
Yarn: 1 skein multicolored sock yarn for 2-3 mm (US 0-3) needles, like Tom Print or Socks from Hjertegarn. One skein is enough for a few small mittens, even socks as well. Einband (The Icelandic laceweight) or other laceweight yarn is used together with the sock yarn for the larger size, 5-6 years old.
Needles: 3 mm (US 3) double pointed needles for the two smaller sizes and 4 mm (US 6) for the largest size where you knit Einband or other laceweight yarn together with the sock yarn.
Gauge: 30 stitches in stockinette stitch with sock yarn and 3 mm (US 3) needles should be 10 cm/4 inches. 20 stitches in stockinette stitch with sock yarn and Einband held together on 4 mm (US 6) needles should be 10 cm/4 inches.

Cast on 28 (32) 32 stitches using 3 mm (US 3) needles or 4 mm (US 6) if knitting the 5-6 year old size with laceweight yarn held together with the sock yarn. Divide the stitches evenly on 4 needles. Join to work in the round and knit 1x1 rib: knit 1, purl 1 for 16 (20) 20 rounds. Now work stockinette stitch for 5 (6) 9 rounds. On the next row make the opening for the thumb. **Right mitten:** knit 2 stitches from the first needle, then knit 4 (4) 5 stitches on to scrap yarn for the thumb opening. Move the scrap yarn stitches back on to the left needle and knit them again with the main color. Knit to the end of the row. **Left mitten:** knit until 6 (6) 7 stitches are left on needle 4, then knit 4 (4) 5 stitches on to scrap yarn for the thumb opening. Move the scrap yarn stitches back on to the left needle and knit them again with the main color. Knit the remaining 2 stitches of the row. Now knit 12 (18) 24 rounds, which should make the mitten long enough. It's a good idea to try the mitten on the hand of its future owner to get a perfect fit. When the mitten is the desired length, it's time to start decreasing for the top. **Decrease row:** needle 1: slip 1, knit 1, pass the slipped stitch over the knit one (skp), knit to end of needle. Needle 2: knit until there are 2 stitches left on the needle, knit 2 together. Needle 3: same as needle 1. Needle 4: same as needle 2. Knit 2 rows without decreasing. Now work a decrease row like before. Knit one round. Next, work the decrease row every row until you have 4 stitches remaining on your needles. Break yarn and pull through the remaining stitches.

Thumb: remove the scrap yarn to pick up the thumb stitches. Divide the stitches on 3 needles. Also pick up two stitches on each side of the opening, to prevent holes, a total of 12 (12) 14 stitches. Knit with four needles 8 (10) 12 rounds. Next row: knit 2 stitches together on each side of the thumb, a total of 4 stitches are decreased. Knit 2 together throughout the next row. Break yarn and pull through the remaining stitches. Weave in all loose ends.

Wash the mittens in luke warm water and then lay them to dry on a towel, gently blocking them into shape. Even the best knitter sometimes makes a mistake and produces two non-identical mittens, but that's nothing a little blocking can't fix, as the old ladies like to say...

Margrét Gauja

Margrét Gauja Magnúsdóttir is a 33 year old teacher and local council member in Hafnarfjörður, a town in the Southwest of Iceland. In this book she is a representative of knitting novices. She began knitting last summer when she felt restless after the end of school term. She posted a note on Facebook asking for someone to teach her how to knit and immediately received many responses from helpful knitters! She started with a simple hat project, that she shares with us here. She has by now knit a couple of dozen hats and has advanced into knitting sweaters as well as embarking on a no-end-in-sight mitten phase. In short, she has become totally obsessed with knitting, and now knits everywhere, including the teacher's coffee room, during council meetings and at home late at night when the children have gone to sleep. She is so enthusiastic about her new hobby, that she has started two knitting clubs. She recently found herself knitting a few stitches while waiting at a red light in a car she herself was driving and she has also forgotten to pick up the kids from preschool, to eat and to bathe, all because she was so eager to finish an ongoing knitting project!

Knitting motto: *If you want to gain control of your mind, simply knit and you will see the world in clear light*

Love Hats

Margrét Gauja calls the hats she knits "Love Hats". She decided to start a "Love Hat epidemic", and so knit these hats for most of the people she loves. Each hat is unique, and Margrét chooses the hat's colors with each person in mind. Her father, for example, got a wine-red and green hat. The wine-red color represented Margrét's old childhood home, and the green represented her father's interest in environmentalism. A good friend of hers got a red and white hat: the red because he's a social democrat, and the white because of his pure heart and soul. Margrét´s own hat is knit with the leftover yarn from many of the hats she's made so far. The love hats are unique, warm and pretty, and those who wear them can't help but feel happy since they can pull the hat down below their ears and block out any annoying noises. For Margrét, there is no end in sight to the Love Hat project since she has alot of friends, many of who are still waiting for their special **Love Hat...**

Margrét Gauja with a Love Hat

Yarn: Dale Freestyle, or Lopi lite for example. Choose colors that you think best represent the person you're knitting for.
Needles: 3 and 4 mm (US 2.5 and 6) 40 cm/16 inches circular needles. Also use 4 mm (US 6) double pointed needles for the last few decrease rounds on the top of the hat.
Gauge: 18 stitches knit in stockinette stitch with the 4 mm (US 6) needles should be 10 cm/4 inches.

Cast on 70 – 100 stitches with 3 mm (US 2.5) circular needles. 70 – 80 stitches are suitable for 2-3 year old children, 90 stitches are good for medium sized heads, and 100 stitches are good for big heads. Join to knit in the round. Knit 2 rows, purl 3 rows. Change to 4 mm (US 6) circular needles and knit love and happiness in stockinette stitch for about 30 rows, or for 10cm/4 inches, in the colors of your choice. It looks nice, for example, to change colors every 5th row. **Decrease** for the top of the head like this: knit 2 stitches together about every 12th stitch. Knit 1 row without decreases. Then knit 2 together every 11th stitch or so, then every 10th, remembering to knit every other row without decreasing. Continue in this manner until about 12 stitches are left. Break yarn and pull through the remaining stitches. Weave in all ends and Presto! Your loved ones will feel warm and happy as they proudly wear your **Love Hat!**

Marín Þórsdóttir is a 32 year old glamour girl and avid knitter and crocheter. She lives in downtown Reykjavík and works for the Icelandic Red Cross. She first learned to knit at six years old when her teacher showed her how it´s done. Her first project was a green garter stitch kitten and, although that was lovely, Marín's projects have only gotten better since. Marín descends from a long line of crafty women and has crocheted a few babtism dresses and knit loads of baby blankets to give to newborns she knows. When she herself was pregnant with her first child she knit five layette sets because she thought none of them was good enough for her unborn son! She says she owes her knitting skills to her mother who used to give her a good talking to if she ever tried to get away with shoddily knit projects. Marín is most creative when using the crochet hook but she just recently started improvising with pattern-free knitting. Like many knitters, Marín goes through periods of obsessive knitting, although her current knitting mania has been going on for almost two years now...

Knitting motto: *It is ok to have one mistake in each garment because it helps remind you that it´s homemade*

Cozy Woolen Stroller Bag

"When my son, Högni, was born, he was given this great stroller, but unfortunately it only came with a thin stroller bag that clearly wasn't made for Icelandic weather conditions. This meant I either had to buy a new and warmer, but very expensive, bag, or I could take the more fun option, get creative and make a warm bag for Högni myself. When this bag was ready I realized that it was much nicer than anything I could have bought in a shop, and also really warm!"

Size: 9 months – 1.5 years. The stroller bag is made rather big so you can dress the baby in warm clothes inside the bag and even leave the bag in the stroller.
Yarn: Lopi lite, 6 skeins in blue, 1 skein in white and 1 skein in grey-brown. Or other yarn of similar weight that gives you the same gauge. Lopi lite is a worsted/light worsted yarn and has approx. 100 m (109 yd)/50 g.
Needles: 4 mm (US 6) circular needles, 60 cm/24 inches long, and double pointed needles. Also 3.5 mm (US E) crochet hook to crochet around the zipper-opening in the front.
Gauge: 21 stitches in stockinette stitch make 10 cm/4 inches.
Other: a zipper for the stroller bag.

The stroller bag is made with holes between the legs for the stroller's safety belt. I made two holes so the bag can "grow with the child." Measure what fits for your stroller. You can close the hole not in use by crocheting a buttonhole on one side and sew a button on the other side. You can also skip one hole and just make one.

Cast on 120 stitches and join to work in the round. Knit until the piece measures 24 cm/9½ inches, then make the holes for the safety belt. **The holes:** knit 25 stitches, cast off 10 stitches, knit 50 stitches, cast off 10 stitches and finish the round by knitting the last 25 stitches. *Next round:* knit 25 stitches, cast on 10 stitches knit 50 stitches, cast on 10 stitches. Now you have two holes for the belt, in the front and in the back of the bag. Now knit 10 cm/4 inches, then repeat the holes if you want to. When the piece measures 40 cm/16 inches increase by making two stitches in the middle in the front of the bag. From now on you always purl these two stitches and they are included in the total number of stitches given in the pattern. These stitches mark the placement of the zipper in the front of the bag as this is where the bag will be steeked and cut open. Knit until the bag measures 65 cm/25½ inches long. Put 6 stitches on each side on a stitch holder; this is where sleeves will be joined to the bag. Now knit the sleeves. **Sleeves:** cast on 30 stitches with 4 mm (US 6) double pointed needles. Join to work in the round and knit rib like this: *round 1:* knit 1, purl 1. *Round 2*: knit. Repeat these two rounds until the rib measures 3 cm/1¼ inches. Now increase 4 stitches evenly spread throughout the next round. Knit 9 rounds. Increase 2 stitches (1 stitch after the first stitch in the round and 1 stitch before the last stitch in the round) every 7th row up the sleeve, 5 times. Now you have a total of 44 stitches on your needles. Knit until the sleeve measures 23 cm/9 inches. Put 6 stitches under the arm on a stitch holder. **Yoke:** join the bag and the sleeves by knitting them on to one long circular needle, placing the sleeves on the sides of the bag for a total of 186 stitches. Knit 1 row. Now knit the **Monkey-pattern** according to the chart on the next page and decrease as shown on chart. Note that the first and the last stitches of the pattern are purled (i.e. the purled stitches in the middle for the zipper are a part of the pattern). When carrying strands across the wrong side of the work for more than 8 stitches at a time, remember to weave the unused strand in as you knit, about midway through the block of stitches, by passing it once over or under the working strand on the wrong side of the work. Knit the last few rounds of the yoke with double pointed needles as it will have become too small for your circular needle. **Neckline:** knit ribbing for the neckline as for the sleeves: *Round 1:* knit 1, purl 1. *Round 2:* knit. Repeat until the rib is 3 cm/1¼ inches, cast off.
Finishing: graft underarm stitches together. Cut the stroller bag open, like this: Using a sewing machine, sew two seams with small stitches in each of the purled stitches down the front of the bag, four seams in all. Carefully cut to open the bag between the two purled stitches. Now work *double crochet** for one row in every other stitch along the cut edges with a 3.5 mm (US E) crochet needle.

Högni enjoying a walk in his warm and cozy stroller bag

Wash the stroller bag and lay to dry before you measure the opening and buy a zipper that fits. Sew the zipper on the crocheted edge with a sewing machine . Weave in loose ends and enjoy the walk with the stroller in the cool weather, knowing your child is warm! If you line the bag with fleece, it will be even warmer and softer...

**Note: We use American English for the crochet terminology. See page 29 for British crochet terms*.*

Marín

Round 34: 60 st on the needle
Round 32: 87 st on the needle
Round 28: 132 st on the needle
Round 17: 150 st on the needle

Note that the first and the last stitch of the monkey pattern is purled (the middle of the bag)

Monkey pattern for the stroller bag

Start here to knit the pattern

Princess Tiara

"Every girl is a princess at some point in her life. During those times, it can be good to have your own tiara, especially your own homemade personal tiara. This tiara was made for a theme-night I had with my girlfriends. The theme was "Royal", and the tiara was made to remind us that we are really all princesses... I recommend that everybody makes their own tiara to use when doing the dishes on the weekend! I've always loved to crochet hair accessories, and it's really easy to make something beautiful with a flower crocheted from leftovers, just by fastening it to a hairpin or a hair band. Just let your imagination run free."

Yarn: gold- or silver colored shiny fine yarn to be used with 2-3 mm (US B-D) crochet hook, like Arista, less than 1 skein.
Crochet hook: 2.5 mm (US B-C) hook
Other: A hair band to fasten the tiara on.
Note: *this pattern uses American English crochet terminology, see page 29 for British crochet terms.*

Start by working 41 chains. *Row 1:* single crochet (sc) in second chain from needle, and then sc in every stitch – 40 sts. *Row 2:* [work single crochet, double crochet, triple crochet, double crochet, single crochet in the next five stitches], repeat this for a total of 8 times. Break yarn, weave in ends. Fasten the crocheted strip with a thread that matches the color of the hair band. Now put the tiara on and enjoy being a **princess...**

Fúsi the Frog

"My friend attended a crochet course and was given a pattern for a very cute rabbit that we've both mass-produced ever since for all the newborn babies around us, in all colors of the rainbow. When I got a bit fed up with the rabbit I started making my own animals, like this little green fellow."

Size: Fúsi is 30 cm/12 inches long, and somewhat chubby (for a frog).
Yarn: Cotton yarn like MOR AASE, Rowan 4 ply cotton, or other cotton yarn of similar weight, 2 skeins in frog green color. And a little bit of white for the eyes, red for the tongue, and black for the eye pupils.
Hook: 2.5 mm (US C) crochet hook.
Note: We use American English for the crochet terminology here***.

Head. Chain 17. *Round 1:* Sc (single crochet) in second chain from hook, sc in each chain across (16 sc), chain 1*, turn. *Round 2:* Sc in each stitch (st) across, chain 1, turn. Repeat this until you have a total of 30 rounds. Fold and sew the sides together.

Eyes, make 2. Chain 2. *Round 1:* work 6 sc in second st from hook. Work slip stitch to join. *Round 2:* 2 sc in each st around – 12 sts. *Round 3:* [sc in next st, 2 sc in next], repeat around – 18 sts. Slip st in first sc to join. *Round 4-6:* Sc in each st around. Break yarn.

Eyelids, make 2. Chain 2. *Round 1:* 3 sc in second chain from hook, chain 1, turn. *Round 2:* 2 sc in each st – 6 sts. Chain 1, turn. *Round 3:* [sc in next st, 2 sc in next st], repeat across – 9 sts. Chain 1, turn. *Round 4:* [sc in each of two next sts, 2 sc in next st], repeat across – 12 sts. Break yarn.

Mouth, make 2. Chain 2. *Round 1:* work 3 sc in second chain from hook. Chain 1, turn. *Round 2:* 2 sc in each st – 6 sts. Chain 1, turn. *Round 3:* [sc in next st, 2 sc in next st], repeat across – 9 sts. Chain 1, turn. *Round 4:* [sc in each of next two sts, 2 sc in next st], repeat across – 12 sts. Chain 1, turn. *Round 5:* [sc in each of next three sts, 2 sc in next st], repeat across – 15 sts. Chain 1, turn. *Round 6:* [sc in each of next four sts, 2 sc in next st],repeat across – 18 sts. Chain 1, turn. *Round 7:* [sc in each of next five sts, 2 sc in next st], repeat across – 21 sts. Chain 1, turn. *Round 8:* [sc in each of next six sts, 2 sc in next st], repeat across – 24 sts. Break yarn. When both mouth pieces are finished, sew them together.

Webbing on hands and feet, make 8. Chain 2. *Round 1:* work 3 sc in second sts from hook. Chain 1, turn. *Round 2:* 2 sc in eac st – 6 sts. Chain 1, turn. *Round 3:* [sc in next st, 2 sc in next st], repeat across – 9 sts. Chain 1, turn. *Round 4:* in each st: [sc, tr, sc], repeat across. Break yarn. Sew two and two pieces together on the "picot edge". The feet and hands are then worked directly from the webbing.

Fúsi the Frog

Feet, make 2. Work directly on to the opening of webbing. *Rounds 1-3:* start on the side of the foot: sc in every st – 22 sts. Chain 1, turn. *Round 4:* sc in each of next 12 sts, turn (time to work the heel). *Round 5:* make 2 sts into 1 sc**, sc in each of next 8 sts, make 2 sts into 1 sc. *Round 6:* sc in each sts around the foot – 20 sts. Work sc in the round until the foot measures 4 cm/1½ inches. Now it is time to make the knee. [Make 2 sts into 1 sc], repeat for a total of 5 times, then sc in each sts that is left of round – 15 sts. Work sc in each st until foot is 8 cm/3 inches.

Hands, make 2. Work directly on the opening of fit. *Rounds 1-2:* Start on the side of the hand: sc in every st – 22 sts. Chain 1, turn. *Round 3:* [make 2 sts into 1 sc], repeat until end of round. Now work sc in each st until hand measures 8 cm/3 inches.

Body. The body is worked in the round, every round ends with a slip st in the first sc to join. Chain 4, join with a slip st. *Round 1:* chain 1, work 6 sc in the ring. *Round 2:* 2 sc in each st – 12 sts. *Round 3:* chain 1, [sc in next st, 2 sc in next st], repeat around – 18 sts. *Round 4:* chain 1, [sc in each of next two sts, 2 sc in next st], repeat around – 24 sts. *Round 5:* chain 1, [sc in each of next three sts, 2 sc in next st], repeat across – 30 sts. Continue like this until you have 54 sts in the round. *Next round:* sc in each st, and now only in the back loop of the stitches (this round only), this will make a small edge that separates the bottom from the back. *Next two rounds:* sc in each st. *Next round:* sc in each of next 17 sts, make 2 sts into 1 sc, sc in each of next 16 sts, make 2 sts into 1 sc, sc in each st until end of round. *Next round, and every other following round:* sc in each st. *Next round:* sc in each of next 16 sts, make 2 sts into 1 sc, sc in each of next 16 sts, make 2 sts into 1 sc, sc in each st until end of round. *Next round:* sc in each of next 15 sts, make 2 sts into 1 sc, sc in each of next 16 sts, make 2 sts into 1 sc, sc in each st until end of round. *Next round:* sc in each of next 14 sts, make 2 sts into 1 sc, sc in each of next 16 sts, make 2 sts into 1 sc, sc in each st until end of round. Continue to decrease number of stitches by 2 in every other round until a total of 32 sts are left. Break yarn.

Tongue. Chain 13, turn. Sc in second chain from hook, and then sc in every st – 12 sts.

Finishing: Sew the parts together and stuff with wool or some other soft filling. Sew all the pieces together: eyes, eyelids and mouth on to the face, and hands, feet and head onto the body.

Give Fúsi to someone that will give him lots of hugs and kisses!

**"I was taught to chain 1 in the end of the row instead of in the beginning of the next row, because it would look nicer to have that stitch a little twisted. This is why I finish the rows with 1 chain, instead of starting the next row that way."*

*** To decrease 2 stitches into 1 is done like this: Insert the hook into the next stitch and pull the yarn through, like you would do when you begin a single crochet. Now insert the hook into the next stitch and also pull the yarn through that one, and then pull the yarn through all three loops on your hook.*

***Crochet terminology

We use American English in our crochet patterns

American English - British English
Single crochet = Double crochet
Half double crochet = Half treble crochet
Double crochet = Treble crochet
Treble crochet = Double treble crochet
Double treble crochet =Triple treble crochet

Good to know...

*Cast on over 2 needles held together so your cast on edge is nice and stretchy. A tight cast on edge can make garments really uncomfortable.

*Oops, did you drop a stitch? Use a crochet hook to retrieve the loop and "crochet" it all the way up to your needles, stitch by stitch.

*Not really sure how to use a stitch marker? Read all about how to mark a stitch on page 24.

*Use hair conditioner to soften your Lopi sweaters. After you've washed them in luke warm water, put hair conditioner in the rinse water – and don't wash it all out.

*Have you joined www.ravelry.com? It is THE online social network for knitters and crocheters. It's a bit like Facebook – except with knitting! It also helps you keep track of your yarn, tools, projects and pattern information, and it's great for browsing for ideas and inspiration.

*Don't hesitate to ask for knitting advice at your local yarnstore or at the next knitcafé.

*If you want more excitement in your knitting, why not use Elizabeth Zimmermann's trick for choosing colors: fill one basket with light colored yarn and another with dark colored yarn, close your eyes and grab yarn from the baskets, alternating between them.

*If you want to brush up on your knitting or crocheting skills, you can find excellent video tutorials online. Try *www.garnstudio.com.*

*Visit our blog at ***www.icelandknits.com,*** where we share knitting and crocheting tips, links to videos and patterns and discuss everything and anything to do with knitting and crocheting.

Ragnheiður

Ragnheiður Eiríksdóttir or Ragga, a 38 year old master knitter, comes from Sauðárkrókur in the North of Iceland, but lives in Reykjavík. She learned to knit when she was around 8 years old and remembers clearly her first self-designed, self-knit project. It was a Santa Claus doll, a little creature knit in the round, wearing a Santa hat, that she remains very proud of to this day. Since then, Ragga has had intermittent periods of knitting, for example during her two pregnancies, when she mostly made hippie-style garter stitch sweaters for her children. Then, when living in Sweden and unable to work for a while due to illness, she took up knitting again along with Halldóra, one of the authors of this book, and quickly became totally obsessed. Since then, knitting has slowly overtaken her life to the point that today she now works full time in the world of knitting, and is overjoyed about getting to do for a living what she loves so much. Ragga always has several knitting projects on the go, and has different projects for different situations, like meetings, lectures, and waiting, a situation she doesn't find to be a problem at all: "Waiting isn't boring if you just knit yourself through it,!" It seems knitters' perception of the passing of time is different from most people's. Check out Ragga's knitting activities at www.raggaknits.wordpress.com and on www.knittingiceland.com.

Knitting motto: *Freedom in knitting comes when you know as many techniques and tricks as possible, because then you realize that there are no limits*

The Candy Raglan

The Candy Raglan is a lightweight sweater knitted in the round from the top down. The Icelandic wool used has unique qualities being airy and warm at the same time.

Sizes: 3-5 (6-8) 9-12 years. Chest circumference 60 (70) 78 cm/23½ (27½) 30½ inches. Sleeve length from neckline: 41 (51) 64 cm/16 (20) 25 inches. Length of body from the neckline: 43 (52) 65 cm/17 (20½) 25½ inches.
Needles: 5 mm (US 8) circular needles, 80 cm/32 inches long, and a set of double pointed needles or a shorter circular needle to knit the narrower shoulder part and the sleeves. Adjust needle size if necessary to obtain the correct gauge.
Yarn: Nammi, handdyed Icelandic laceweight Einband, 80 (100) 130 g, or other laceweight yarn that gives you the same gauge. The Icelandic laceweight has approx. 229 m (250 yd)/50 g.
Gauge: 20 stitches and 26 rows = 10 cm/4 inches.
Other: 9 stitch markers

To mark a stitch: *Put a stitch marker on your needle before the stitch you want to mark, knit the stitch and put another marker on your needle on the other side of the stitch. Note that the stitch marker hangs on the needle and is lifted from left needle to the right every time you come to it in your knitting. Make sure that you only have one stitch between each 2 markers in this project. The markers are there to remind you that the increases are always to be made on both sides of the same middle raglan stitch.*

Increases: choose either one of the following increase methods

1. The M1 method creates a symmetrical and almost solid increase. (M1R): knit to a stitch marker, lift the strand of yarn between the needles up on the left needle by bringing the left needle under the yarn from the back, knit into the front of the strand, lift the stitch marker over to the right needle, knit the middle stitch, lift the second marker over to the right needle, (M1L): lift the strand between the needles up on the left needle by bringing the left needle under the yarn from the front, knit into the back of the strand.

2. The yarn over (YO) metod creates a symmetrical open increase and the holes formed by the YO´s can add a nice decorative touch to the raglan: knit to a stitch marker, make a YO, move the stitch marker, knit the middle stitch, lift the second stitch marker, make a YO, knit on. On the next round knit into the YO´s as if they were regular stitches.

One over two bind-off: knit the first 3 stitches, pass the first knitted stitch over the other two on the needle. Knit 1 more stitch, pass the stitch to the far right over the other two on the needle. Repeat until 3 stitches are left – pass the 2 right stitches over the 1 to the left, break the wool and pull the end through.

Now, lets knit the Candy Raglan: cast on 76 (80) 88 stitches. Join to work in the round and place a marker at the beginning of the round. The beginning is in the middle of the back. Round 1: knit 13 (13) 14 stitches, M1R (or YO), place marker, knit 1, place marker, M1L (or YO), knit 10 (11) 13, M1R (or YO), place marker. Knit 1, place marker, M1L (or YO), knit 26 (27) 29, M1R (or YO), place marker, knit 1, place marker, M1L (or YO), knit 10 (11) 13, M1R (or YO), place marker, knit 1, place marker, M1L (or YO), K13 (14) 15. Round 2 and all even numbered rounds: knit all stitches. Round 3: knit to the first marker, *M1R (or YO), move the marker to the right needle, K1, move the marker to the right needle, M1L (or YO), knit to the next marker, repeat from *. Alternate rounds 2 and 3 until you have increased the number of stitches to 188 (224) 264, a total of 14 (18) 22 increase rounds. **Now set the sleeve stitches aside:** knit to the first marked stitch, *remove the first marker, knit the marked stitch, remove the second marker. Now put the 38 (47) 57 sleeve stitches on to scrap yarn. Cast on 3 (4) 6 stitches onto your right needle (use the backward loop method or cable cast on) and continue knitting the stitches off the left needle, removing the 2 markers on each side of the first stitch*. Knit way to the next marked stitch and repeat the process from *to*. Now continue knitting the body. Round 1 of body: Locate the 2 middle stitches on each side of the body under the arms and place markers on each side of them in the first round. Every 6th round: work M1 increases on either side of the marked side stitches in the sides, a total of 4 stitches are increased/round. Work the increases for a total of 7 (9) 14 times. Continue knitting until the sweater measures about 43 (52) 65 cm/17 (20½) 25½ inches. Cast off using the "One over two bind-off" method. This type of casting off makes a cute gathered edge that doesn't roll. **Knit the sleeves:** start by putting the sleeve stitches for one of the sleeves on your knitting needles. Knit the first round, but when you come to the "new" stitches under the arm, pick up 3 (4) 6 stitches from the underarm cast-on, also pick up 1 stitch on each side of them, a total of 5 (6) 8 new stitches. Knit until end of round. In the second round, knit 2 stitches together a total of 3 times under the arm. Now continue knitting until the sleeve measures about 41 (51) 64 cm/16 (20) 25 inches measured from the neckline. Cast off using the one over two bind-off method. Knit the other sleeve the same way. Weave in all ends... you're done!

Rúna Lóa wearing The Candy Raglan

Guðrún

Guðrún Axelsdóttir is 55 year old super-duper knitter from Hafnarfjörður in the South of Iceland. She learned to knit and crochet back in school, and to this early exposure she credits her excellent knitting skills today: "Everybody had to learn to knit back then". She's an experienced knitter and no knitting pattern is too difficult for her. Guðrún is the kind of knitter who can't watch TV without knitting. She knits regularly for the whole family, designs her own socks, mittens and hats for the winter, as well as knitting and crocheting georgeous sweaters and blankets. She not only knits for her own family, but picks up her needles whenever she hears of a pregnant woman, be she friend, family or acquaintance, and knits something for the un- or newborn baby. She knit all her christmas presents last year, and it looks like the same will happen this year...

Knitting motto: *I'd be bored to death if I didn't have my knitting!*

Long Cabled Cardigan

"I wanted a long Lopi cardigan, but one different from the traditional Icelandic patterned yoke construction – so I came up with this one instead, since I've always loved cables." This cardigan is very warm and cosy, with its longer-than-average length and high collar, and it's really beautiful! This is THE cardigan for winter.

Size: medium (large). Chest measurement (when laid flat) under the sleeves: 98 (106) cm/38½ (42) inches, lenght from the neck down: 83 (86) cm/ 32½ (34) inches. Sleeve length: 46 (48) cm/18 (19) inches.
Yarn: Icelandic unspun wool, light gray, 500 (600) g, or other yarn of similar weight that gives you the same gauge. The Icelandic unspun has approx. 300 m (328 yd)/100 g.
Needles: 8 mm (US 11) circular needles, 40 and 80 cm/16 and 32 inches long, a cable needle, and a 4.5 mm (US 7) crochet hook size 4,5 (US 7)for the buttonbands. Adjust the needle size if necessary to obtain the correct gauge.
Gauge: 12 stitches in stockinette stitch make 10 cm/4 inches.
Other: you also need 8 buttons.

Body: cast on 124 (132) stitches and join to knit in the round. This sweater is knit in the round and then steeked and cut open to become a cardigan. The first and last stitches of each row form the middle of the front of the sweater and are purled up the whole body, as that is where the sweater will be steeked. The two purled stitches are not counted when number of stitches is given hereafter. Start by knitting ribbing like this: Row 1: knit 1, purl 1, repeat to end of row. Row 2: knit. Repeat these two rows for 9 cm/3½ inches. After that, knit this pattern: Purl 5, knit **"The cable pattern"** over the next 24 stitches, knit "**Pattern 1**" over the next 20 (24) stitches, knit "The cable pattern" again over the next 24 stitches, knit "Pattern 1" over the next 20 (24)

Dina happy and warm in the Long Cabled Sweater

stitches, knit „The cable pattern“ once again over the next 24 stitches, purl 5 stitches = 122 (130) stitches. This pattern is repeated until the body measures 63 (65) cm/ 25 (26) inches. Now set the body a side and knit the sleeves. **Sleeve:** cast on 32 (34) stitches and work rib as for the body for 9 cm/3½ inches. On the last row, increase 8 (10) stitches = a total of 40 (44) stitches. Knit pattern 1 until the sleeve measures 46 (48) cm/18 (19) inches. Place 10 stitches (underarm stitches) on a stitch holder. Knit the other sleeve. **Yoke:** continue to knit the pattern and join body and sleeves like this: knit right front piece; 26 (28) stitches. Place 10 stitches of the body on a stitch holder (they will be grafted together with 10 stitches from the sleeve later). Knit 1 sleeve; 30 (34) stitches, knit the back of the sweater; 50 (54) stitches, place 10 stitches on a stitch holder. Knit the other sleeve; 30 (34) stitches, then the left front piece; 26 (28), a total of 162 (178) stitches. **Row 1: decrease row:** continue to knit the pattern over the next 23 (25) stitches (right front), skp (slip 1, knit 1, pass the slipped stitch over the knitted one), knit 2, knit 2 together. Knit the sleeve stitches; 24 (28), skp, knit 2, knit 2 together. Knit the back; 44 (48), skp, knit 2, knit 2 together. Knit the sleeve stitches; 24 (28), skp, knit 2, knit 2 together. Knit the left front; 23 (25), skp, knit 2, knit 2 together. **Row 2:** knit. Repeat these two rows (with 8 stitches decreased every other row) 12 (14) times, leaving a total of 66 stitches. Continue to knit the pattern for 2 more cm/0.8 inches, then knit the collar. **Collar:** work rib as for the body over the 63 stitches for 12 cm/4½ inches, bind off loosely. To give the collar more character, you can knit the collar with heavier yarn, like Álafoss bulky lopi. In the sweater pictured, I used some bulky handspun wool. **Finishing:** Graft the underarm stitches together. Cut the sweater open, like this: Using a sewing machine, sew two seams with small stitches in each of the purled stitches up the front of the sweater, four seams in all. Carefully cut to open the sweater between the two purled stitches. **To make buttonbands; Note:** *this pattern uses American English crochet terminology, see page 29 for British crochet terms.* Work single crochet (sc) with a 4,5 mm (US 7) hook, in about every other knit stitch along the cut edge. Crochet 3-4 rows to make the buttonbands. Crochet 8 buttonholes in one of the buttonbands in the third crochet row like this: Chain 2, skip 2, (sc) in the third stitch. The top and bottom buttonholes are placed 2 cm/¾ inches away from the top/bottom edge, and the others are placed evenly in between. Weave in all ends and sew buttons on to the buttonband. Hand wash in luke warm water, rinse with hair balsam to make the cardigan extra soft, lay to dry.

Long Cabled Cardigan - Cable pattern

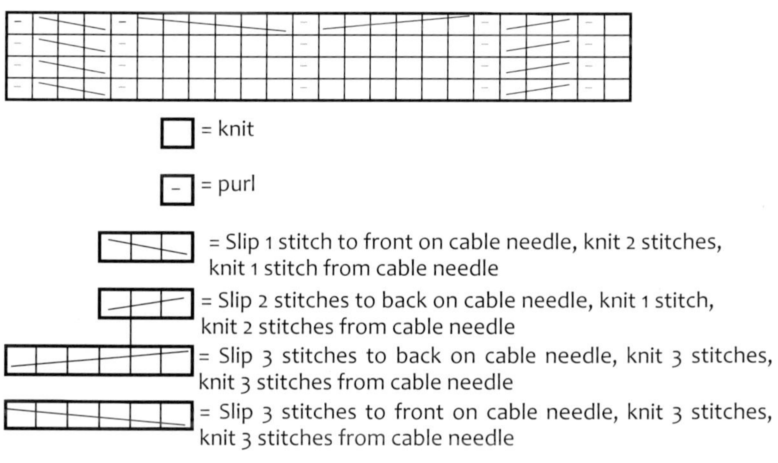

Pattern 1:

Row 1: [knit 1, purl 3], repeat around
Row 2: knit 2, purl 1, [knit 3, purl 1], repeat around

Guðrún

Vera's Cute Granny Square blanket

"I made this blanket for my grandchild Vera when she was born. The blanket kept her warm when she slept outside in her baby carriage or went for a walk with her parents . It is very easy to change the size of this blanket; you can just add squares to it until it's the size you want."

Size: each square is about 12.5-14 cm/5-5½ inches wide. This blanket is made of 30 squares, and it is 90 x 110 cm/35½ x 43½ inches large.
Yarn: Lopi lite, in the colors you like, and white is used around each square. A total of 600 g of Lopi lite was used for this blanket. You can also use other yarn of the same weight, Lopi lite is a worsted/light worsted yarn, and has approx. 100 m (109 yd)/50 g.
Crochet hook: 4.5 mm (US 7).
Note: *this pattern uses American English crochet terminology, see page 29 for British crochet terms.*

One square: chain 8, join with a slip stitch in first chain. *Round 1:* chain 3 (turning chain, counts as first double crochet), work 15 double crochet (dc) in ring and join with a slip stitch in third chain of turning chain. *Round 2:* [chain 6, skip next dc, join with a slip stitch in next dc], repeat around, end by joining with a slip stitch in first stitch – a total of 8 loops. *Round 3:* make a "flower petal" in each loop: sc, hdc (half double crochet), 2 dc, hdc, sc. Join with a slip stitch in first sc to end round. *Round 4:* work 3 slip stitches to get to the top of the flower petal. [Chain 8, work dc on top of next flower petal, chain 3, work dc in same stitch (corner of the square). Chain 8, work sc in top of next flower petal], repeat around, join with a slip stitch in first stitch to end round. *Round 5:* chain 3 (counts as first dc), work 5 dc in next loop. Now work in the corner loop of the square: 3 dc, chain 3, 3 dc. [In the next loop: 6 dc, 1 dc in the sc, 6 dc in the next loop. In the corner loop: 3 dc, chain 3, 3 dc], repeat around. Join with a slip stitch to end the round. *Round 6:* chain 3 (counts as first double crochet), and then dc in each dc 7 times, or until you come to the corner. [Dc 3, chain 3, dc 3 in the corner, then dc in each dc, a total of 19 times], repeat around. Join with a slip stitch to end the round. Break yarn. *Round 7:* change to white color and chain 3 (counts as first dc). Work dc in each dc until you come to the corner, then [work 3 dc, chain 3, work 3 dc in the corner, and then dc in each dc until you come to next corner], repeat around. Join with a slip stitch to end round.

Crochet 30 squares, or as many as you would like to have in your blanket. When all the squares are ready, sew them together with white yarn. Crochet a border around the whole blanket like this: Start by joining white yarn on the edge with a slip stitch. *Round 1:* [chain 5, skip the next 3 stitches, sc in next stitch], repeat around. Join with a slip stitch to end round. *Round 2:* work 2 slip stitches in the loop. [Chain 1, 5 dc in next loop, chain 1, sc in next loop], repeat around. Join with a slip stitch to end round. Weave in all loose ends.
Now, let this beautiful blanket keep you warm!

Perla

Crochet terminology
We use American English
in our crochet patterns

American English - British English
Single crochet = Double crochet
Half double crochet = Half treble crochet
Double crochet = Treble crochet
Treble crochet = Double treble crochet
Double treble crochet =Triple treble crochet

Guðrún

Hekla

"I made this sweater for my granddaughter Hekla. Sweaters made with 1 strand of Icelandic unspun wool are warm and flexible - perfect for children. I wanted to design a lightweight and colorful sweater with a simple yoke pattern. The sweater Hekla is the result. I'm really happy with the colors, as I think they suit Hekla´s temperament very well. I find choosing the colors for children´s sweaters one of the most enjoyable parts of each project."

Size: 1.5-2 (3-4) years old.
Yarn: Icelandic unspun wool, 100 g red and about 50 g of each: yellow, brown, white, or other yarn of similar weight and gives you the same gauge. The Icelandic unspun wool has approx. 300 m (328 yd)/100 g.
Needles and hooks: 4.5 mm (US 7) circular needles, 60 cm/24 inches and double pointed needles, as well as 4 mm (US G) crochet hook. Adjust needle size if necessary to obtain the correct gauge.
Gauge: 18 stitches in stockinette stitch with 4.5 mm (US 7) needles make 10 cm/4 inches.
Other: you also need 5 buttons.

Body: cast on 113 (125) stitches, do not join. Knit stockinette stitch for 4 rows (knit on right side, purl on wrong side). Now knit 1, and then knit eyelet row: [knit 2 together, yarn over], repeat to end of row. Now cast on 2 stitches, they will be placed in the middle of the front and purled up the whole body, and are not counted in the total number of stitches given hereafter. Join to work in the round, knit 5 rows. Knit pattern from chart 1; start knitting the pattern where the arrow indicates. Then knit with main color until the piece measures 20 (24) cm/8 (9½) inches from the eyelet row. Now knit the sleeves. **Sleeve:** cast on 28 (32) stitches, join to knit in the round, place marker to indicate start of row. Knit 4 rows, then knit eyelet row: [knit 2 together, yarn over], repeat to end of row. Knit 5 rows, increase 4 stitches evenly spread in the last row = 32 (36) stitches. Knit pattern 1, making sure the beginning of the pattern is under the sleeve so the jog between different colored rows is less visible. After the pattern, knit and increase 2 stitches under the arm in every 6th row until the stitches are a total of 42 (46), a total of 8 (10) increases. Knit with main color until the sleeve measures 21 (26) cm/8 (10) inches from the eyelet row. Place 5 (6) stitches under the arm on a stitch holder. Knit the other sleeve. **Yoke:** join body and sleeves like this: Knit right front; 26 (28) stitches, place 5 (6) stitches on a stitch holder. Knit one sleeve; 37 (40) stitches, knit back; 51 (57) stitches, place 5 (6) stitches on a stitch holder. Knit the other sleeve; 37 (40) stitches, knit left front; 26 (28) stitches = a total of 177 (193) stitches. Knit pattern from chart 2 and decrease 9 (7) stitches evenly spread over the first row = 168 (186) stitches. Change to shorter needles as the yoke gets smaller. After chart 2 you should have 53 (61) stitches on the needles. **Neckline:** knit 3 rows. Bind off the two purled stitches in the middle of the front piece. Now knit eyelet row: Knit 1, [knit 2 together, yarn over], repeat until end of the row. Knit 3 rows back and forth (knit on right side, purl on the wrong side), bind off loosely. **Finishing:** graft the underarm stitches together. Fold the edges on body, sleeves and neck and fasten to create a picot edge. Weave in all ends. Cut the sweater open, like this: Using a sewing machine, sew two seams with small stitches in each of the purled stitches up the front of the sweater, four seams in all. Carefully cut to open the sweater between the two purled stitches. **Right front buttonband:** crochet with a 4 mm (US G) crochet hook and 1 strand of Icelandic unspun. **Note:** *this pattern uses American English crochet terminology, see page 29 for British crochet terms. Row 1:* single crochet (sc) in about every other knit stitch on the cut edge. *Row 2:* single crochet in every stitch. *Row 3:* Make 5 buttonholes: The first and last one 1.5 cm/0.6 inches from the top/bottom edge, and three evenly spread there in between. Single crochet in every stitch, but to make buttonholes, chain 2, skip 2 stitches, single crochet in the third stitch and then sc in every stitch until next buttonhole. Row 4: sc in every stitch. **Left front:** *row 1:* single crochet in about every other stitch on the cut edge. *Row 2 and 3:* work single crochet in every stitch. Weave in all ends, fasten buttons on to buttonband. Hand wash in luke warm water, rinse with hair balsam to make it softer, lay to dry.

Chart 2

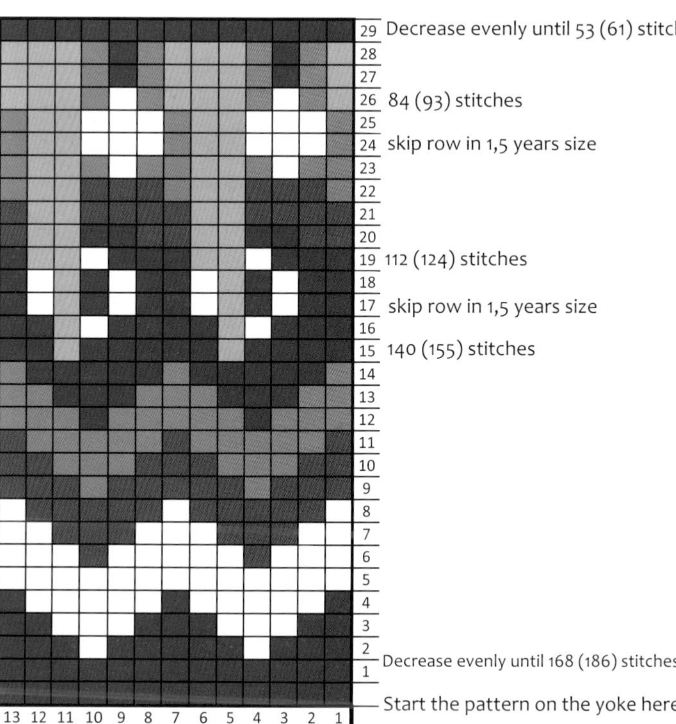

Chart 1

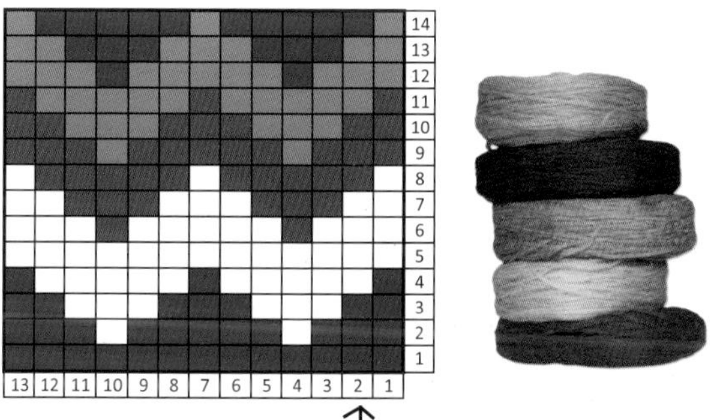

Start knitting the lower pattern on the cardigan and on sleeves

Berglind Dýrleif wearing Hekla

Elsa

Elísabet Matthíasdóttir is a 62 year old multitalented handicraft enthusiast from Siglufjörður in the North of Iceland. She learned to knit back in school and fondly remembers her very strict Danish arts & crafts teacher: "She constantly pushed us to work harder, smacked our fingers with a stick if she didn't like our work, and we weren't even allowed to go to the toilet during her classes!" Elsa fortunately did well in the class and was one of the teacher's favourite students. She remembers being 12 years old and doing complicated needlework and various crochet projects like wash cloths, baby sweaters, doll's clothing and crocheting around coat hangers. She first started to crochet these little baby booties when she was pregnant with her first child, who is now 40 years old. She crocheted like mad during the pregnancy, and everything in pink – so fortunately for her the baby was a girl! "I've never followed crochet patterns, and I still don't. And I have to be really sick or something not to have anything on the needles."

Knitting motto: *I unravel until I am happy with my project – my grandmother taught me that*

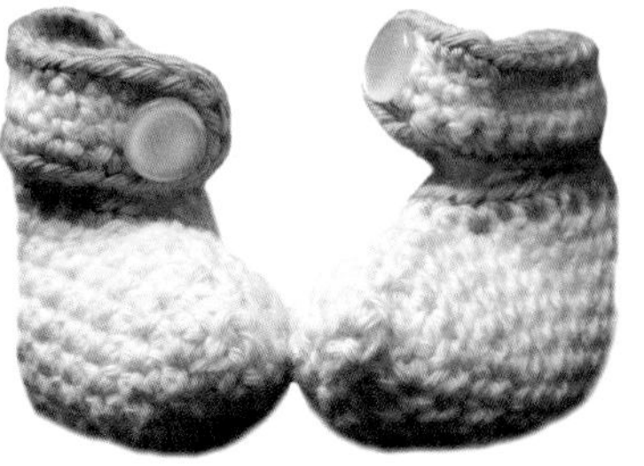

Crocheted Baby Booties

"I've made these booties for every baby born around me for so many years, and I even have them "in stock". They are so simple and are such a cute and fun present. You can easily decorate them with something beautiful sewn on, to make them even more personal."

Size: 0-6 months
Yarn: fine cotton yarn for a crochet hook size 3-4 (US D-G). Scrap yarn in another color to decorate the booties.
Crochet hook: 3.5 mm (US E)
Note: *this pattern uses American English crochet terminology. See page 29 for British crochet terms.*

Chain 30, turn. *Round 1:* single crochet (sc) in third stitch from hook, and then sc in every stitch across – 28 sts. Chain 1, turn. Repeat round 1 with sc in every stitch until the piece measures 8 cm/3 inches. Now decrease on the next 4 rounds by skipping stitches evenly spread until you have 8 stitches left on the round. Break the yarn, thread on to a tapestry needle or blunt darning needle, thread through the remaining 8 stitches and pull to close, this will form the toe of the booties.

Ankle straps: chain 30. Turn and work sc in third loop from hook, and then sc in every stitch across – 28 sts. Chain 1, turn. Repeat round 1 with sc in every stitch twice more. Make a buttonhole on one side of the band: Chain 5-6 stitches on one end of the strap and fasten with a slip stitch.

Finishing: fold the piece to form a flat bootie, sew the pieces together for about 5 cm/2 inches on the top of the foot, and sew the bootie together on the back of the heel. Work sc with yarn in another color around the opening of the booties and also around the straps. Fasten a button on the ankle strap and then fasten the middle of the strap itself with a few stitches on to the back of the bootie. Fasten the straps so that the buttons and buttonholes face oposite directions. To finish, sew something cute lika a flower or stars on the side of the bootie.

Vilborg María

Vilborg María Ástráðsdóttir is a 34 year old farmer and mother of four from Skarð in Hreppar in the South of Iceland. She thinks her interest in knitting might have started because she used to freeze when riding her horses, but found that on a cold day nothing beats sweaters and socks made from the Icelandic wool, Lopi. She has convinced her four children from birth that the Lopi is not scratchy. Vilborg María also works as a preeschool director and has created a special knitting culture for her staff: „If we get a new employee, he will begin knitting within 2 weeks of starting work with us - if he doesn't knit already". She encourages all parents to dress their children in Lopi sweaters, socks, and mittens. And if a child is short of wooly clothes they have a good Lopi clothing stash at the preeschool to lend out! Vilborg learned to knit at school, but only became obsessed with knitting about 2 or 3 years ago. She has always been inspired by her grandmothers, and also by her mother-in-law who is a self-proclaimed „knitting maniac" – and now Vilborg has followed in her footsteps. Vilborg´s youngest child is 5 months old, so her knitting time is mostly late in the evening and into the night. She uses every chance she can get to knit and regrets all time spent on household chores, since she would of course much rather be knitting! She has become quite proficient at multitasking, and can cook, change diapers, breastfeed and knit at the same time! She also never travels in a car as a passenger without knitting, as that would be a waste of good knitting time! Read more about Vilborg´s knitting adventures on her blog: www.lopinn.blogspot.com.

Knitting motto: *Knitting rewards with joy*

Little Brown Bokki

"The little ones need warm and nimble clothing and this little Lopi sweater, made with 1 ply Icelandic unspun, fulfills those requirements. It's easy to knit with 1 ply of the Icelandic unspun wool, but you have to be gentle with the thread and not in a bad mood, since it is, as you might know, quite fragile. For added strength, you can knit it together with Einband (Icelandic laceweight), but check your gauge if you do and adjust the needle size, or the number of stitches you cast on. This pattern is quite versatile and can, with small adjustments, produce a variety of sweaters. The only limit is your own imagination. Here the pattern is partly knit with purled stitches which gives a definite character to this lovely little sweater."

Sizes: 6-12 months (1-2 yrs). Chest measurement (when laid flat): 24 (27) cm/9½ (10½) inches, total length: 31 (34) cm/12 (13½) inches, sleeve length 20 (23) cm/8 (9) inches.

Yarn: 1 ply Icelandic unspun wool, dark brown for the main color, approx. 100 g. Light grey and light blue for the pattern, just a few grams of each color. Or other yarn of similar weight that gives you same gauge.The Icelandic unspun has approx. 300 m (328 yd)/100 g.
Needles: 3.5 (US 4) and 4 mm (US 6) double pointed and circular needles, 40 cm/16 inches long. Adjust needle size if necessary to get the correct gauge.
Gauge: 19 stitches in 1 ply Icelandic unspun and 4 mm needles in stockinette stitch = 10 cm.

Body: cast on 93 (99) stitches with 1 ply unspun Icelandic in gray on 3.5 mm (US 4) circular needles. Change to dark brown, join to knit in the round and work rib for 15 rows like this: [knit 1, work 2 sts in seed/moss stitch*], repeat until end of row. When the ribbing is finished, change to 4 mm (US 6) circular needles, increase 1 stitch and work in stockinette stitch until body measures 20 (23) cm/8 (9) inches. **Sleeves:** cast on 33 (36) stitches with 1 ply unspun Icelandic in gray on 3.5 mm (US 4) double pointed needles. Change to dark brown yarn, join and work rib as for the body for 15 rows (knit 1, work 2 sts in *seed/moss stitch**, repeat until end of row). Change to 4 mm (US 6) needles and work in stockinette stitch (no increasing, the sleeves are straight) untill the sleeve is 20 (23) cm/ 8 (9) inches. Place 6 underarm stitches on a stitch holder, they will be grafted together with 6 stitches from the body in the end. Knit the other sleeve. **Yoke:** join body and sleeves as follows: place 6 stitches on each side of the body on a stitch holder for the underarms. Knit the first sleeve (except the 6 underarm stitches) on to the circular needle to be joined with the body. Knit 41 (44) stitches of the body for the front of the sweater. Knit the second sleeve (except the 6 underarm stitches). Knit 41 (44) stitches for the back. Now knit the pattern and decreases according to the chart. The pattern repeat is 4 stitches, so the total number of stitches has to be divisible by 4. In the last row of the chart, decrease the number of stitches evenly through the row so you have a total of 60 (66) stitches. Now work rib as for the body (knit 1, work 2 sts in *seed/moss stitch**, repeat) for 9 rows. Change to gray and work 9 more rows of ribbing. Bind off loosely. Fold neckline to inside with 1-2 rows of gray ribbing showing, and fasten loosely with a tapestry needle. Graft underarm stitches together and weave in loose ends. Rinse sweater by hand in lukewarm water and lay flat to dry. Weave elastic thread in the ribbing in the neckline to keep it snug. This is done since the neckline is made rather large so the sweater is easy to put on and take off.

**Seed/moss stitch: knit 1, purl 1, and on the next row do the opposite: purl 1 on top of a knit stitch, knit 1 on to of a purl stitch.*

Vilborg María

Buttercup
in a field of grass

"These woolen socks are knit with Lopi lite and two threads of Einband, the Icelandic laceweight held together. The cuffs are long to keep the legs warm, and to keep the sock on the foot. These socks are for example good for babies carried in a sling or a wrap, where the feet stick out. In the cuff I knit partly from the wrong side to give it a different texture. I was inspired by Icelandic nature when knitting these socks; the grass, the moss, and the beautiful buttercups."

Size: 6-12 months (1-2 years).
Yarn: Lopi lite, 1 skein moss green and Einband (Icelandic laceweight) in light green, part of 1 skein. Or other yarn of similar weight that gives you same gauge. Lopi lite has approx. 100 m (109 yd)/50 g. And a little yellow leftover yarn as well to sew buttercups on the socks.
Needles: 3.5 mm (US 4) double pointed needles. Adjust needle size if necessary to obtain the correct gauge.
Gauge: 18 stitches in stockinette stich make 10 cm/4 inches.

Cast on 33 (39) stitches with Lopi light, divide the stitches evenly on 4 needles and join to knit in the round. Knit 7 (10) rows of ribbing like this: knit 1, knit 2 stitches *seed/moss stitch**. Now turn the piece to work from the wrong side, and knit 4 rows with two threads of Einband (Icelandic laceweight), this will look like garter stitch on the right side. Decrease 3 stitches in the

last row by knitting 2 together evenly spread. Turn the piece to work from the right side again. But before you turn, knit 1 row with the Lopi lite. Now work 7 (10) rows of ribbing like before. After that, turn the piece to work from the wrong side again and knit 4 rows with 2 threads of Einband held together as before. During the last row decrease 3 stitches evenly spread. Before turning the piece back to work from right side again knit 1 row with Lopi lite. Now knit 7 (10) rows of ribbing from the right side. Knit 5 (8) rows in stockinette stitch, and increase 1 stitch in the first row in the smaller size, and decrease 1 stitch in the larger size (yes, doesn´t sound logical – but it's the way it should be) = 28 (32) stitches. Now knit the heel. **Heel:** adjust the stitches so there are 14 (16) stitches on one needle (the heel stitches), and now knit stockinette stitch across the heel stitches only: knit on the right side and purl on the wrong side for 14 (16) rows. Now **turn the heel:** start on a wrong side: purl 9 (10) stitches, purl 2 together, turn. Slip 1, knit 4 (4) stitches, slip 1, knit 1, pass slipped stitch over the knit one, turn. *Purl 4 (4) stitches, purl 2 together, turn. Knit 4 (4) stitches, slip 1, knit 1, pass slipped stitch over the knit one, turn. Repeat from * until 6 stitches are left on the needle, end on the right side. Now pick up 7 (8) stitches along the right edge of the heel flap. Knit across the instep stitches, and pick up 7 (8) stitches on the left edge of the heel flap. **Shape gussets:** divide the stitches evenly on 4 needles. The round starts on the back of the heel. *Needle 1:* knit until 2 stitches are left on the needle, knit 2 together. Knit across instep stitches (*needle 2 and 3*). *Needle 4*: slip 1, knit 1, pass slipped stitch over the knit one. Knit 1 row. Repeat these two rows until 7 (8) stitches are left on each needle. Work these stitches for 7 (10) more rows. **Shape toe:** Switch to two threads of Einband held together and knit 1 row. Purl 1 row. Needle 1 (the row starts in the middle under the foot): knit until 3 stitches are left on needle, knit 2 together, knit 1. Needle 2: knit 1 stitch, slip 1, knit 1, pass slipped stitch over, knit to end of needle. Needle 3: knit like needle 1. Needle 4: Knit like needle 2. Knit 1 row. Repeat these two rows until a total of 8 stitches are left on the needles, then knit 2 and 2 stitches together for 1 row. Break yarn and pull it through the remaining stitches. Weave in all ends. U**sóleyju.**p yarn to sew a little **buttercup** on the instep of the sock. Knit the other sock.

**Seed/moss stitch: knit 1, purl 1, and on the next row do the opposite: purl 1 on top of a knit stitch, knit 1 on top of a purl stitch.*

Hrafnaklukka

"When I was little I really liked hrafnaklukka (Lady smock, *Cardamine nymanii*), the delicate violet little flowers you can find all over Iceland. I used to pick them and give to my mother, and she would put them in a glass of water on the table. When knitting this sweater I was inspired by Icelandic nature, the gray basalt, and the beautiful violet flower, hrafnaklukka. This sweater is very simple; both body and sleeves are straight up to the yoke with no increases or fuss. It is quite wide, and if you make the body long it could be used as a dress, with trousers or leggings."

Sizes: 1.5–2 (3-4) 5-6 years.
Yarn: the main color is knit with 1 ply of Icelandic unspun wool, and Einband (Icelandic laceweight) held together. You need approx. 200 g Icelandic unspun and 50 g Einband for all sizes. You can knit the yoke pattern with either 2 strands of Einband held together, or with 1 ply Icelandic unspun and 1 strand Einband held together, in colors of your choice. I did it like this: dark violet: Icelandic unspun + Einband in same color, light violet: Einband, 2 strands held together, light pink: Einband 2 strands held together, white: 1 strand Icelandic unspun + 1 strand Einband. For the pattern you need just 1 skein of each color. Icelandic unspun wool has approx. 300m (328 yd)/100 g, and Einband, the Icelandic laceweight has approximately 229 m (250 yd)/50 g. You can also use other yarn of similar weight that gives you same gauge.
Needles: 3.5 mm (US 4) and 4 mm (US 6) double pointed and circular needles, 40 and 60 cm (16 and 24 inches) long. Adjust needle size if necessary to obtain the correct gauge.
Gauge: 16 stitches in stockinette stitch with 1 ply Icelandic unspun and 1 thread Einband held together on 4 mm (US 6)

Body: Cast on 120 (132) 144 stitches with 1 ply Icelandic unspun wool and Einband held together in main color using 3.5 mm (US 4) circular needles, join to knit in the round. Work rib for 15 rows, like this: [knit 1, work 2 sts in seed/moss stitch*], repeat until end of row. After the rib, change to 4 mm (US 6) circular needles and work in stockinette stitch until body measures 32 (38) 42 cm /12½ (15) 16½ inches. Now knit the sleeves. Sleeves: cast on 42 (51) 60 stitches with main colour on 3.5 mm (US 4) double pointed needles. Join and work rib as for the body for 15 rows (knit 1, work 2 sts in seed/ moss stitch*). Change to 4 mm (US 6) needles, and increase 2 (1) 0 stitches = 44 (52) 60 stitches. Work in stockinette stitch (no increasing, the sleeves are straight) until the sleeve is 26 (30) 34 cm/10¼ (11¾) 13½ Inches long. Place 6 (7) 8 underarm stitches on a stitch holder, they will be grafted together with stitches from the body in the end. Knit the other sleeve. **Yoke:** join body and sleeves like this: place 6 (7) 8 stitches on each side of the body on a stitch holder for the underarms. Knit the first sleeve (except the 6 (7) 8 underarm stitches) on to the circular needle to be joined with the body. Knit 54 (59) 64 stitches of the body for the front of the sweater. Knit the second sleeve, except the underarm stitches. Knit 54(59) 64 stitches for the back. Now you should have a total of 184 (208) 232 stitches on your needles. Place a marker to indicate the beginning of the row, and now work pattern and decreases from the chart as indicated. Start with knitting 5 (7) 9 rows as shown, then work the decrease round as follows: starting with the back of the sweater, knit 19 (19) 19 stitches, then knit the decreases. **Decreases:** [knit 3 stitches together like this: slip 1 stitch knitwise, knit 2 stitches together, pass the slipped stitch over the new stitch. Knit 2 stitches]. Repeat this decrease 5 (6) 7 times, then knit the rest of the back of the sweater. **The first sleeve:** knit 18 (19) 21 stitches, then knit the decreases 2 (3) 4 times, knit the rest of the sleeve. The front is worked like the back, and the second sleeve like the first sleeve. Now you should have 156 (172) 188 stitches on your needles. Work the pattern according to the chart. Bind off loosely. Graft underarm stitches together and weave in all loose ends. Rinse sweater by hand in luke warm water and lay flat to dry. If wished, weave elastic thread around the edges of the neckline and cuffs.

**Seed/moss stitch: knit 1, purl 1, and on the next row do the opposite: purl 1 on top of a knit stitch, knit 1 on top of a purl stitch.*

Vilborg María

Hrafnaklukka - pattern

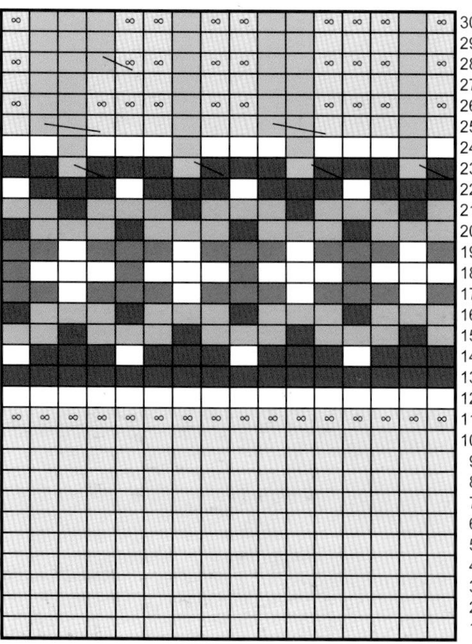

- 30 Purl and cast off
- 28 Purled row. Change to needles 3.5 mm (US 5). Decreases: 9th and 10th stitches are knit together
- 26 Purled row
- 25 Decreases
- 23 Decreases
- 11 Purled row
- 10 Decrease row
- 7 1-2 (3-4) yrs: skip row
- 6 1-2 (3-4) yrs: skip row
- 5 1-2 yrs: skip row
- 4 1-2 yrs: skip row

Perla

> Knitting came to Iceland with German, English or Dutch traders in the early 16th century. Knitted garments soon became Iceland's main export commodity and remained very valuable to the economy until the late 18th century.

Grámhildur the Good

"This cardigan is a classic and I wouldn´t be surprised if it became your favorite. It is light and airy since it is knit with Lopi lite. Take good care of it and it will be with you for a long time. You can play around with the pattern as you like and for example make the cardigan longer, wider, turn it into a pullover, or use a zipper instead of buttons. You could knit the yoke in a different color – how about that? Maybe you would like to use ribbing rather than garter stitch for the bottom of the sweater? Or crochet around the edges? Make your own version of Grámhildur the good."

Size: medium- large. But it is easy to shorten and adjust the lenght of the sleeves, as well as the lenght of the body to make it a size medium. Chest measurement (when laid flat) under the sleeves: 43 cm/17 inches, lenght from neckline to lower edge: 59 cm/23 inches, sleevelenght under the arm: 48 cm/19 inches.
Yarn: Lopi lite, 5-600 g in dark gray. Lopi lite is a worsted/ light worsted yarn, and has approx. 100 m (109 yd)/50 g.
Needles: 5.5 mm (US 9) circular needles, 40 and 80 cm/16 and 32 inches long, as well as double pointed needles. Adjust needle size if necessary to obtain the correct gauge.
Gauge: 15 stitches in stockinette stitch make 10 cm/4 inches.
You also need 6 buttons.

Body: cast on 144 stitches with 5.5 mm (US 9) needles. The first and last stitches of each row form the middle of the front of the sweater and are purled up the whole body, as that is where the sweater will be steeked and cut to become a cardigan. If you would like the sweater to be a pullover, cast on only 142 stitches and skip the two purled stitches in the middle. Do not join, knit 2 rows. Knit lace-band; [knit 2 together, yarn over] to end of the row. Purl 1 row. Knit 2 rows. Now join to knit in the round and knit stockinette stitch untill the body measures 38 cm/15 inches. Place 8 stitches on each side of the body on a stitch holder for the underarms. Now knit the sleeves. **Sleeve:** cast on 47 stitches and knit a garter and lace border just like the border on the body of the sweater, and then join and knit stockinette stitch in the round. Increase 3 stitches (= 50 stitches) in the last 10 cm of the sleeve, and knit until the sleeve measures 48 cm/19 inches. Place 8 sleeve stitches on a stitch holder. Knit the other sleeve. **Yoke:** now join body and sleeves on one needle, place the sleeves on the sides of the sweater with the two purled stitches in middle of the front of the sweater. Now you should have a total of 210 stitches (the two purled stitches are not counted). Knit the pattern from the chart, and then bind off loosely. **Finishing:** graft the underarm stitches together. Cut the sweater open, like this: using a sewing machine, sew two seams with small stitches in each of the purled stitches up the front of the sweater, four seams in all. Carefully cut to open the sweater between the two purled stitches. Pick up stitches to knit the buttonbands one at a time. Ideally, you should pick up 2 stitches for each three rows of the cardigan. For the band without buttonholes, knit 8 rows in garter stitch and then bind off. For the buttonhole band: knit 4 rows then make holes for the buttons by knitting 2 stitches together and then making a yarn over. If you have large buttons you need to bind off 2-3 stitches, and then cast on 2-3 stitces in the next row. The buttons are placed 2 cm/¾ inch from the top and bottom edges, and the other 4 are evenly spread there inbetween. You can also crochet the buttonbands if you like. Then you would work a single crochet in every other stitch for 3-4 rows. Crocheted buttonholes are made by chaining two, skipping two stitches and working a single crochet in the third stitch. Weave in all ends, handwash the sweater in lukewarm water and lay to dry.

Vilborg María

Grámhildur´s Pattern Chart

x								x						x						51	Purled row, bind off
																				50	Knit row
O								/						O						49	Lace-band (knit 2 together, yarn over), repeat until end of row
x								x						x						48	Purled row
																				47	Here you should have a total of 64 stitches left
																				46	Decrease
																				45	Decrease
																				44	Decrease
																				43	
																				42	
																				41	
																				40	
																				39	
x	x			x	x			x	x	x	x			x	x			x	x	38	
																				37	
x	x			x	x			x	x	x	x			x	x			x	x	36	Row 36: 126 stitches left
																				35	
	O			Δ	O						O			Δ	O					34	
																				33	
O	/				\			O		O	/				\			O		32	
																				31	
/									O	/								\	O	30	Decrease
x	x		x	x	x		x	x	x	x	x		x	x	x		x	x	x	29	
																				28	
x	x		x	x	x		x	x	x	x	x		x	x	x		x	x	x	27	
																				26	
																				25	
			O	Δ	O								O	Δ	O					24	
																				23	
	O		/		\		O				O		/		\		O			22	
																				21	
O	/						\	O		O	/						\	O		20	
																				19	
									O	/									O	18	Decrease
x	x	x	x	x	x	x	x	x	x	x	x	x	x	x	x	x	x	x	x	17	
																				16	
x	x	x	x	x	x	x	x	x	x	x	x	x	x	x	x	x	x	x	x	15	
																				14	
			O	Δ	O								O	Δ	O					13	
																				12	
		O	/		\	O						O	/		\	O				11	
																				10	
	O	/				\	O				O	/				\	O			9	
																				8	
O	/						\	O		O	/						\	O		7	
																				6	
/									O	/									O	5	
x	x	x	x	x	x	x	x	x	x	x	x	x	x	x	x	x	x	x	x	4	
																				3	
x	x	x	x	x	x	x	x	x	x	x	x	x	x	x	x	x	x	x	x	2	
																				1	

- Δ Slip 1, knit 2 together, pass the slipped stitch over
- \ Slip 1, knit 1, pass the slipped stitch over
- / Knit 2 together
- o Yarn over
- x Purl 1

Perla

Knitted garments were a very important export commodity in Iceland for centuries. In the year 1764 Icelanders exported more than 250 thousand pairs of socks and in 1806 about 280 thousand pairs of mittens!

The Icelandic Lopi Sweater - *Lopapeysa*

Lopapeysa or the Lopi sweater is an Icelandic hand knit sweater characterized by its circular yoke design. It is believed that the sweaters were originally inspired by traditional Greenlandic women's costumes, or even South American, Swedish and Turkish textile patterns. Even though the Lopi sweater is closely identified with Iceland, it's a relatively recent phenomenon, originating as late as in the 1950s.

This book contains some patterns for traditional Lopi sweaters, like *Hekla* and *Bokki*, both of which children's patterns. Other Icelandic Lopi sweater patterns in the book are *Hrafnaklukka, Grámhildur* and the *Monkey Cardigan,* all sweaters based on traditional patterns but with a modern twist.

About 90% of Icelanders have one or more Lopi sweater. This isn't surprising because - let´s face it – on a cold day (and there are plenty of those in Iceland), nothing beats a sweater made with Lopi wool. It's the warmest of all wool. Recently, it has also become quite a fashion statement...

Þorgerður

Þorgerður Pálsdóttir is a 29 year old engineer living downtown in Reykjavík. In her spare time she does yoga, rides her bike and sews and knits. She usually knits in front of the TV, and when travelling as a passenger in car. Þorgerður was 7 years old when her grandmother, who was well known for her craftsmanship, taught her how to knit. When she was 11 years old she spent a weekend at her grandmother's house doing little else than knitting. There she managed to finish her school knitting assignment and showed it proudly to the teacher when she got back to school on Monday. The teacher became angry and told her that she shouldn't let anyone else finish the knitting assignments for her! Þorgerður usually has several ongoing knitting projects, and knits a lot of baby stuff for her friends when they have babies. She also steps in if someone needs an Icelandic Lopi sweater, or a pair of mittens .... she's NEVER knit anything for herself!

Knitting motto: *Don´t think twice about frogging, as it will keep you from having to face your mistakes forever*

Cabled Hat

"The idea of this hat came up when I was talking to my sister, who is also very interested in design and clothes. We wanted a hippie style hat with cables, and this was the result, after two attempts. The first hat was not knit with Lopi, but after I switched to the Lopi I was much happier with the results, and the fact that the wool is Icelandic makes it even better."

Size: medium.
Yarn: Lopi lite, 100 g. 2 skeins, or other yarn of similar weight that gives you the same gauge. Lopi lite is a worsted/light worsted yarn, and has approx. 100 m (109 yd)/50 g.
Needles: 4.5 mm (US 7) needles, both circular 40 cm/16 inches long, and double pointed. For the cables, a cable needle would be useful. Adjust needle size if necessary to obtain the correct gauge.
Gauge: 18 stitches in stockinette stich = 10 cm/4 inches.

Cast on 92 stitches, join and knit 6 rows of 2 x 2 ribbing (knit 2, purl 2). Now increase 13 stitches evenly spread over next row and start the cable pattern. **Cable pattern:** *[purl 1, knit 6, purl 1, knit 13], repeat until end of row. Knit 8 rows like this. Next row, make the cables: [purl 1, put the next 3 stitches on a cable needle or extra needle held in front, knit 3, now knit the 3 stitches on the cable needle. Purl 1, knit 13], repeat through the row.* Repeat from *-* untill the hat measures 24 cm/9½ inches, bind off. **Finishing:** thread a blunt darning needle with the yarn, and thread it through the bound off edge on top of the hat (thread with about 2 cm space between the stitches). When you have threaded yarn around the whole hat, pull until the hat tightens at the top and the hole closes. Sew a few stitches on the wrong side to be sure to close the hat. Weave in all ends.

Ilmur Dögg

Ilmur Dögg Gísladóttir is a 32 year old knitter with a punk approach and a devoted interest in all forms of knitting. What got Ilmur knitting again after a long break were not the traditional Icelandic Lopi sweaters, but rather skull-patterned pot holders that she found online. Ilmur originally learned to knit at school, where she completed the mandatory assignments. Then, when she was about 16 years old, her mother taught her to knit a raglan sweater, which was the only thing Ilmur would knit for the next few years, in all sizes and colors and shapes. Ilmur shares the basic pattern for this sweater here with us. A few years ago, Ilmur liked to improvise with her knitting, but unfortunately the result often turned out to be a disaster. She was about to give the whole thing up in frustration when she discovered the Stitch'n'Bitch books and the vibrant world of online knitting. This reignited her passion for knitting, and taught her to use patterns and even to add her own designs to them: „Then everything suddenly worked out! " Check Ilmur's knitting blog at www.prjona.net.

Knitting motto: *I don't have only one single knitting motto, because for me knitting is a lifestyle!*

Summer Shawl

Ilmur Dögg

"This shawl is inspired by The Blue shawl (Blár skakki) by Margrét Gísladóttir, from the book *Three cornered and long shawls* by Sigríður Halldórsdóttir. I started the shawl because I wanted a simple project to work on during my summer vacation, and I had a lot of Einband (Icelandic laceweight) leftovers. I love colors and don't like knitting with only one color, so this project was perfect for me as Einband comes in so many beautiful colors. The rows of eyelets in between the color-changes give the shawl a really interesting and cool look. The shawl was a present for a good friend of mine and she uses it equally for weddings and more mundane situations, like going out for a walk. You can wear the shawl in many ways; like a neckerchief, throw it over your shoulders or even tie it behind your back the old fashioned way."

Yarn: Einband (Icelandic laceweight) or other laceweight yarn. You could also try to mix yarn of different weights and fibers, like Lopi and kid silk mohair for example.
Needles: 4- 4.5 mm (US 6-7) circular needles.

The shawl is knit in garter stitch, apart from the middle stitch which is purled on all odd-numbered rows. In every other row the number of stitches is decreased by 4, by knitting 2 together on both sides of the middle stitch and near the edges of the shawl.

Cast on 417 stitches. Place stitch markers on each side of the middle stitch. *Row 1:* knit all stitches, except the middle stitch which is purled. *Row 2:* knit 3 stitches, knit 2 together, knit until 2 stitches before the middle stitch, knit 2 together, slip marker, knit the middle stitch, slip marker, knit 2 together, knit until 5 stitches are left of the row, knit 2 together, knit 3. Repeat rows 1 and 2 to make the shawl. When changing colors, the first row of the new color is an eyelet row, knit like this: [knit 2 together, yarn over], repeat until the end of the row. If the eyelet row is an even numbered row, remember to decrease in the middle and at the edges of the shawl. You can change colors as often as you like, just switch to the next color when you are tired of the one you are working with, thats how I do it! When only 7 stitches are left, break yarn and pull it through the remaining stitches. Weave in all ends. Wash the shawl in luke warm water and block.

The Icelandic wool

The Icelandic sheep is quite unique.
It's one of the world's oldest and purest breeds of sheep, protected by natural isolation. Its fleece has two layers, a distinctive combination of inner and outer fibres, which each produces different kinds of wool. The outer layer is water-repellent and is made up of long, tough fibres called tog, while the inner layer is highly insulating and cold resistant and is made up of finer, softer fibers called þel (pronounced thel). The two fibres are blended together in Icelandic knitting yarn, combining the different qualities of the two layers, making it ligther, warmer and more water repellent than other wool. A further striking characteristic of the Icelandic sheep is its natural colours, which come in shades of black, grey and brown as well as the usual white. Together, these create the distinctive look of Icelandic knitwear, one of the best-known examples of which is the Lopi sweater. The Icelandic unspun can be worked one, two or more strands at a time, depending on how bulky a yarn you want. Gently wind the required number of strands together into a ball by taking one end from the center and one end from the outside of the wheel, or wheels, you're working with. Because the fibres are not spun tightly, the Icelandic wool breaks easily, but fortunately it's also easy to repair the breaks. You can get good results with joining two pieces of yarn together by splicing. Felting works well for that same reason. The structure and texture of Lopi wool means it will easily form a matted, felted surface, so take care when washing and drying knitted garments that you don't want to felt...

Ilmur Dögg

"When I was 16 years old I learned to knit a raglan sweater and since then I've made these sweaters in all possible sizes and shapes. Their charm lies in their simplicity and the fact that they look good on everybody. I have made them in both children and adult sizes, slim-fitting as well as loose, and in all types of yarn, from the laceweight Einband to Bulky Lopi. I often make them striped, and sometimes the sleeves don't even match. Knitting this sweater is super simple. Usually I just estimate the number of stitches to cast on by thinking something along the lines of: „Well, this is approximately the size I want this sweater to be, so I guess this is the right number of stitches..."

Simple Sweater in all Sizes

- with raglan sleeves

Chose some yarn and suitable needles. Cast on a sufficient number of stitches for the body and join to knit in the round. For me, knitting with Lopi lite, I need approximately 200 stitches for the body, and 60 stitches for each sleeve. For a child: 120 stitches for the body, and 40 stitches for the sleeves. Knit the body of the sweater in the round up to the sleeves (you could measure the length of a sweater you have that fits you well). For this sweater I started with a 2x2 ribbing (knit 2, purl 2), so the edges wouldn´t curl. When the body is ready, cast on a sleeve and knit until it's long enough. Make two. I make my sleeves straight, without increases, and rather wide. Now join the sleeves with the body. Place the sleeves on the sides of the body, with equally many stitches in the front and the back piece. Place 8 stitches on a stitch holder on each side of the body, as well as 8 stitches on each sleeve. These are the underarm stitches and will be grafted together once all the knitting is done. Join body and sleeves on one long circular needle. Mark the four body stitches that are closest to the join where the sleeves meet the body, a total of 4 markers. Knit 4 rows. Then begin the raglan sleeve decreases: *Row 1:* knit 2 stitches together on each side of the marked stitch. Purl the marked stitch. A total of 8 stitches are decreased on each decrease row. *Row 2:* knit 1 row. Repeat rows 1 and 2 until you feel the neckline is the right size. Then knit a few rows of ribbing so the neckline won't curl. Bind off loosely. I usually make the necklines of my sweater rather wide. Weave in all ends, and graft the underarm stitches together. Instead of purling the marked stitch between the raglan decreases, you can just knit the stitch, or knit 2 stitches, or even leave no stitch between the decreases, or any other variation you can think of. They will all give the sweater a different look.

This is the perfect sweater to knit with your favorite yarn.

1. Find your gauge by working out how many stitches you have in each cm/inch when knitting with your yarn of choice: Cast on about 25 stitches with needles suitable for your yarn. Knit several rows in stockinette stitch (or whatever stitch/pattern you plan to use for your sweater). Grab a tape measure and measure how many stitches you have in 10 cm/4 inches. For Lopi lite for example knitted on 4.5 mm (US 7) needles, the gauge is usually about 18 stitches over 10 cm/4 inches = 1.8 stitches per cm or 4.5 stitches per inch.
2. How wide do you want the sweater to be? You could measure your favorite sweater that fits you well. Lets say it is 100 cm/40 inches in circumference.
3. 100 cm x 1.8 = 180 stitches/40 inches x 4.5 = 180 stitches: you need to cast on 180 stitches :) Follow Ilmur's instructions, and use the same method to find out how many stitches to cast on for the sleeves.

Pom Anhborg, 32 years old, is Halldóra´s neighbour in the Northern suburbs of Stockholm, Sweden. She is really enthusiastic about her crafty hobbies. „This is the best thing that's happened to me – apart from my three children", she says about knitting and crocheting. „I never could have imagined how great this is! " She learned to knit and crochet in school many years ago, but wasn't so interested in crafts at that age and soon forgot all she'd learned. Then she recently taught herself to crochet again with help of YouTube videos on the internet, but her first finished project was very special and didn't actually look like either knit nor crochet but rather like a technique of its own. „I like crochet more than kniting because I feel it's easier to work with only one needle, and the technique makes me feel more free than knitting does. I don't follow patterns much, at least not yet." It's only been 9 months since Pom learned to crochet and knit (again), but now she's totally obsessed, and uses every spare moment for her new hobby. She's started a knitting blog, and she also started a knit-café in her neighbourhood. Check out her knitting blog at: www.madebypom.blogspot.com.

Knitting motto: *"It's alive!" – That's what I say about my creations if they're a bit deformed or otherwise not perfect*

The Little Lamb

This little lamb is so sweet! And kids love to carry it around for hugging, cuddling and playing. It's both knitted and crocheted, mostly from curly yarn.

Size: the lamb is about 34 x 20 cm/8 x 13½ inches.
Yarn: curly lamb wool-like yarn for the body: here Puddel from Drops, 1 skein in dark gray, and 1 skein Baby Eco ull from Marks & Kattens in white for the head, or other sport weight yarn.
Needles and hooks: 5 mm (US 8) circular needles or long needles (double pointed needles are too short for this project). And 4 and 6 mm (US G and J) crochet hook.
Note: *this pattern uses American English crochet terminology, see page 29 for British crochet terms.*

Start with the body. It's just a knitted square, and the legs are crocheted directy on to it. **Body:** the body is about 17 x 22 cm/ 7 x 9 inches. Cast on 24 stitches with gray curly lamb wool-like yarn on 5 mm (US 8) needles, do not join. Knit garter stitch back and forth for 40 rows, or for as long as you want the body to be. Cast off. Pom crocheted little "bumps" on to the sides of the body of the lamb by working a few double crochet around the edges, to make it look more like lamb's skin. Now crochet the legs. **Right hind leg:** with 6 mm (US J) crochet hook and the gray curly yarn, work 7 double crochet (dc) from the corner towards the centre of one of the shorter edges of the knitted square, 1 in each stitch. Crochet two more rows like this on top of each other. In the fourth and last row: work a dc only in every other stitch = a total of 4 dc. **Left hind leg:** work 5 dc from the other corner and towards the centre on the same edge of the square as before, 1 in each stitch. Crochet two more rows like this on top of each other. **Note:** the hind legs are not identical. **The front legs:** work 6 dc from the corner towards the centre of the other short edge of the square for the first front leg. Repeat this row on top of the first. Third row: skip every other st. Work 3 dc. Work the other front leg in the same manner from the other corner. **Tail:** work 4 dc on the edge between the two hind legs, 1 crochet stitch in each knit stitch. *Next row:* skip 1 dc in the middle – 3 dc. *Last row:* single crochet (sc), dc, sc. **Head:** use the white yarn and 4 mm (US G) crochet hook. Chain 3, join with a slip stitch in the first chain. *Round 1:* work 6 sc in the ring. *Round 2:* work 2 sc in each stitch (st) – 12 sts. *Round 3:* [sc in next st, 2 sc in next st], repeat around – 18 sts. *Round 4:* [sc in each of next two sts, 2 sc in next st], repeat around – 24 sts. *Round 5:* [sc in each of next three sts, 2 sc in next st], repeat around – 30 sts. Repeat this until you think the head is big enough, or 7-8 cm/2½ – 3 inches. Then work half double crochet (hdc) in every stitch for 5 rounds. Now work sc and decrease by skipping every 5th stitch until about 20 stitches are left. Now fill the head with wool or other soft filling before the opening gets to small. Crochet a few more rows with decreasing number of stitches to close the opening. **Ear, make 2.** Chain 10 with the white yarn and 4mm (US G) crochet hook. Work triple crochet (tc) in second stitch from needle, tc in each of next two sts, dc in each of next two sts, hdc in each of next two stitches, and sc in the last st, turn. Work sc in each stitch around the whole ear, also on the first tc on the edge of the ear as well as on the chained stitches on bottom of the ear. Break yarn. **Eyelids, make 2.** Chain 3, work 6 dc in third st from hook. Break yarn. To assemble, it is best to start with sewing the head on to the body, and then place the face on the head by sewing eyes, nose and mouth on to the face. Try to place the face so that the lamb is looking up when lying on its belly. Sew the eyelids and ears on to the head, and crochet curly hair on to the head by working sc with the curly yarn. Start by working sc around the face, and work to the back of the head. Weave in all ends – it's ready!

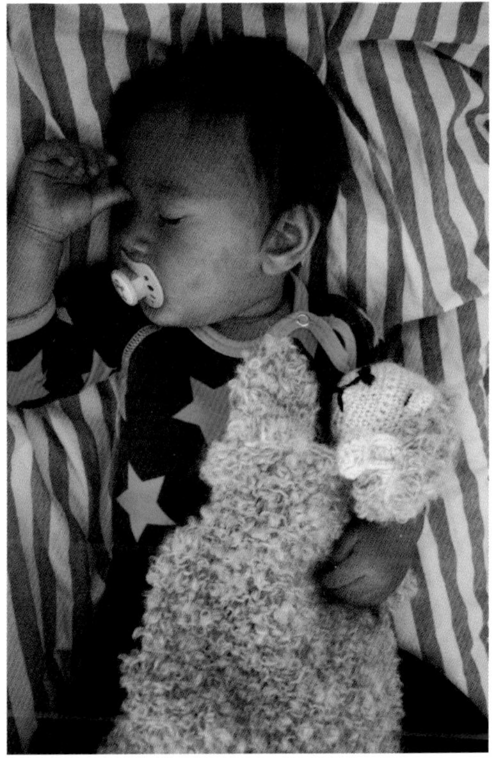

Frank asleep with his little lamb

Perla

The earliest documentation of crochet is from around the year 1800. There is some indication that people did crochet before that, using a bent forefinger in place of a crochet hook.

Emelía

Emelía Kristbjörnsdóttir is 83 years old and totally hooked on knitting. She was born in Skeiðar in the South of Iceland, where she later married the boy from the farm next door and moved in with him, so she never actually left home. It was her mother who originally taught her how to knit, but Emelía hated it until she was 18 years old! She preferred doing the outdoors work, and didn't see the point of sewing, doing needlework and knitting– until one day when she became totally obsessed with it. Back then there was no TV or radio, so all of people's spare time could be used for needlework and knitting. She began to knit, crochet and hairpin crochet, and is still going strong. Today, she spends most of her day knitting various projects, mostly socks, mittens, hats, hens and seals (!), and also teaches elderly people how to knit. She loves all kinds of knitting patterns, and likes to make up her own. "If I see a pattern I like, I usually want to try and improve on it."

Knitting motto: *To knit as many patterns as possible*

TV mittens with traditional ribbed cuffs.

TV Mittens

Here you get a fun version of the traditional Icelandic TV Socks, but they've been changed into mittens! "I've knit many pairs of TV Socks in my days, but I never actually liked the way the instep looked. So I developed this color pattern from a traditional Icelandic Lopi sweater and knit it on to the socks. My friend then suggested I knit mittens using this same method, and so I did and it worked very well. As well as knitting this color pattern on to TV Socks and mittens, I have also knit it on to all kinds of hats, ear warmers and vests."

Size: medium (large). Length: 26 (29) cm/10¼ (11½) inches, width: 10,5 cm/4 inches. You can get children sized mittens (10–12 years old) by knitting the medium size with Lopi lite on 3.5 mm (US 4) needles.
Yarn: Icelandic unspun wool, 2 strands held together. Icelandic unspun has approx. 300 m (329yd)/100 g.For the pattern given here you need white and two shades of blue.
Needles: 4 mm (US 6) long needles, or circular needles, 40 cm/16 inches long.
Gauge: 16 stitches in stockinette or garter stitch should be 10 cm/4 inches.

These mittens are knitted back and forth, lenghtwise. You start by knitting the stockinette stitch part on back of the hand, followed by the garter stitch part in the palm of the hand. When finished, the mitten is sewn together lengthwise. You can either knit a garter stitch cuff at the same time you knit the mitten itself (see the brown and

TV mittens with garter stitch cuffs.

white mittens), or you can knit a traditional ribbed cuff by picking up stitches around the mitten's opening and knitting a regular 1x1 rib (see the blue and white mittens). Cast on 27 (32) stitches with white yarn, using the long tail cast on method. You start by knitting the

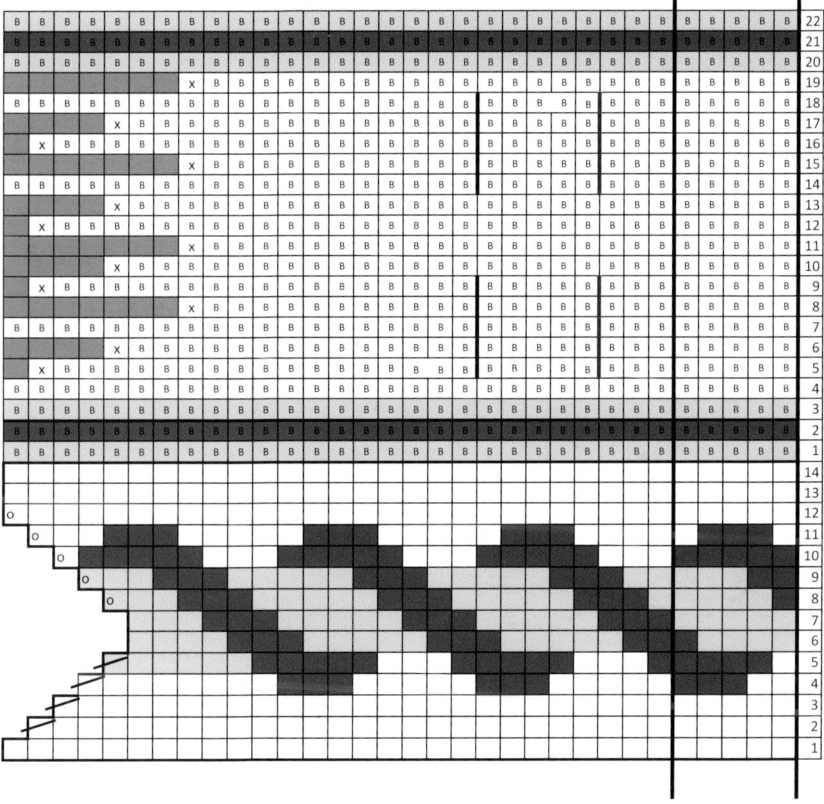

Size M, start here, 27 sts

Size L, start here, 32 sts

back of the hand by following the pattern from the chart. Knit on the right side and purl on the wrong side for stockinette stitch. Note: in the chart for the stockinette stitch part on the back of the hand, 1 square equals 1 stitch, but in the chart for the garter stitch part in the palm of the hand, each square on the chart equals two rows. In the third row you start decreasing on the left side of the piece. This is done to narrow the mittens at the top. When past the middle of the back of the hand you start increasing again on the left side. Either by working a regular increase, or by picking up stitches where you decreased them before – which will save you sewing this part together in the end. The garter stitch in the palm of the hand has a few short rows, shown as **"x"** in the chart, which means that you should not knit this row any further, but turn. To prevent holes in the short rows it's a good idea to make a yarn over before you turn, and then in the next row, knit the yarn over together with the next stitch. When it's time to make the thumb opening, do it like this: knit 8 stitches from the wrist, turn (see thick line on the chart that indicates where the thumb should be placed. Red line: size large, black line: medium size). Leave the other 19 (24) stitches on a spare needle or stitch holder, and knit the 8 stitches on the working needle back and forth for a total of 10 rows. Then knit the other 19 (24) stitches for 10 rows as well, and leave the previously knit 8 stitches on a spare needle or stitch holder. When 10 rows have been knit on both sides of the thumb opening join the stitches by knitting them all on to one needle. Knit according to the chart, and when finished you can either cast off and sew the mitten together lenghtwise, or you can pick up stitches on the cast-on side of the mitten, using a separate needle, and bind them off with the live stitches using the three needle bind off. That's done like this: turn the mitten inside out. Knit 1 stitch from each needle together, repeat so you have 2 stitches on your right needle. Now cast off on the right needle by passing the right stitch over the left one. Repeat this for all the stitches. **Thumb:** pick up 15 stitches around the thumb opening, divide them evenly on to 3 needles and knit 12-14 rows. Now knit 2 together throughout one row, break yarn and pull through the remaining stitches. **Regular 1x1 ribbed cuff:** when the mitten itself is finished pick up 28 – 30 stitches on the edge of the mitten's opening and knit a ribbed cuff; knit 1, purl 1 for about 7-8 cm/2½ -3 inches. Bind off very loosely. It's pretty to knit 2-3 rows in the cuff with a different color. **Garter stitch cuff:** the garter stitch cuff is knit at the same time as the mitten itself. When casting on, cast on 14 extra stitches in the same color as you intend to knit the palm with, so cast on a total of 41 (46) stitches. Always knit the first 14 stitches in garter stitch, and without color changes. When changing colors, take care to wrap the cuff yarn together with the new color to prevent holes. About every 14th row in the cuff is knit shortened, for a total of 4 short rows in the cuff. This means that when knitting on the wrong side (from mitten to cuff), you only knit 1 stitch from the garter stitch part, then turn. This is done to make the cuff a little narrower.

Knit - 1 line in pattern chart = 1 row

B *Garter stitch - 1 line i pattern chart = 2 rows*

Knit 2 together

o *Increase by 1 sts*

x *Short row: decreases*

Rán

Rán Ingvarsdóttir is a 31 year old lawyer from Hafnarfjörður in the Southwest of Iceland. She is completely unfamiliar with knitting terms and doesn't follow patterns. That doesn't stop her from knitting though! She began to improvise with needles and yarn when she was pregnant with her daughter 2 years ago and found it impossible to stop. Her crafts teacher at school, who originally taught her to knit, was not impressed with how averse she was to following rules and patterns. When instructed to make a sweet-looking, blonde doll in a pretty dress, Rán made a chubby doll with braces on her teeth and red hair. While the teacher wasn't happy, Rán loved the doll and hung it on her wall where it stayed for many years. Rán herself is a bit puzzled by how resistant she remains to knitting patterns...

Knitting motto: *Just keep on knitting; it always turns out to be something in the end!*

Knitted Critters

When making the Knitted Critters I love the feeling of total freedom! I enjoy knitting them just the way they "come to me" and seeing how they take shape as I knit. When children come over to visit, they like to play with the Critters, and my daughter Gerða carries her Critters around all day long and gives them plenty of hugs. She has other, "prettier" dolls, but the Critters are still her favorites. Who can blame her? Just look at them, filled with so much personality and character :)

Rán's Knitted Critters are a great example of how a beginner, knitting without a pattern, can find an outlet for her creativity. In this case, the result is a fun project – a "not-so-perfect" creature, that's still so perfect somehow. The Critters are simple to make and actually totally freestyle as they can take any shape - almost... Pick up the needles and give it a try. What does your Critter look like?

Material: choose some soft yarn in any color you like. This is also a great project for leftovers. Choose needles appropriate for your yarn. You also need some wool or other kind of filling, and a tapestry needle.

Gerða with her Critters

The Critters are made from 6 knitted squares. One for the head, one for the body, and the rest for the arms and legs. The size of the squares depends on how you want your Critter to be shaped. I just cast on a few stitches, and knit a few squares in garter stitch, and a few in stockinette stitch - I like to mix textures in one and the same Critter. Then I stitch a face on to the square that's to become the head. I sometimes sew buttons on for the eyes, or use something else I find lying around the house. It's totally okay if the eyes don't match. Next, I use yarn to stitch the mouth and nose on to the face. I sometimes like to knit the nose: I just knit a small square, sew it together so it becomes like a round ball, stuff it with filling, and sew it on to the face. Then I sew the squares together, to form a head, body and limbs, and stuff them with filling. The pieces are then sewn together to form a Critter. You can also knit ears or a tail for your Critter to give it some extra character...

Happy Critter knitting!

Perla

Gauge

Gauge =

Number of stitches in cm/inch

We know that this little word is loathed by many knitters, especially those too impatient to spend time on knitting a little square when they could just get started with the sweater itself. But swatching can save you sweat, tears, frustration – and a lot of frogging! No one wants to spend hours knitting a sweater that doesn´t fit...

Your gauge swatch tells you whether you knit loosely or tightly. It tells you how many stitches YOU have in every cm or inch with your selected yarn and needles. This can vary hugely between knitters, as some produce loose stitches while others knit so tightly, they end up with fabric that's almost waterproof... If your gauge is not the same as the one given in the pattern you risk ending up with a garment that doesn't fit. Try changing your needle size until you get the specified gauge. Use larger needles if you have too many stitches per 10 cm/4 inches, and smaller needles if your stitches are too few.

Once you get a hang of measuring your gauge, you can easily knit your own specially designed sweater – that fits! Turn to page 45 to read about how you can use your favorite yarn to knit a raglan sweater without a pattern.

Kristrún

Kristrún Eiríksdóttir is 60 years old and lives in Egilsstaðir in the East of Iceland. Apart from knitting, her main hobbies are hiking and any other kind of outdoor activity taking place in the beautiful Icelandic landscape. However, her knitting is never far away, and she uses every spare minute to add stitches to her projects. She clearly remembers her first serious knitting project, undertaken when she was only 12 years old. She embarked on knitting a sweater in brioche stitch for herself – not a particularly easy project. She had knit the body all the way up to the underarms when her mother, a passionate and experienced knitter, noticed a mistake and made her unravel the whole thing! Understandably, this was not an easy task for the novice knitter, and she shed some tears while frogging. Despite the adversity, Kristrún didn't give up, but started all over again and ended up with a beautiful sweater! As a child, Kristrún also remembers playing with her mother's old hand-cranked sewing machine, much to her mother's chagrin, as the machine became a bit unreliable after these experiments. However, with this machine Kristrún sewed her first things, for example beautiful clothes for her dolls.

Knitting motto: *It will look better after blocking!*

Mittens from Egilsstaðir

"I got the idea for these mittens from the 1985 edition of *Hugur og hönd*, the annual magazine published by *The Icelandic Handicrafts Association*. In it, I found a small photo showing wristwarmers knit with a lace pattern similar to the one used in these mittens. The photo's caption said that the wristwarmers were knit in 1970, copying ones knit in the first half of the 20th century. The lace pattern is called *rósastrengsprjón* in Icelandic."

Size: medium.

Yarn: Einband, Icelandic laceweight, 40 g. You can choose whichever colors you like for these mittens. I often like to use three colors, as shown in the top mittens in the photo: The darkest color for the cuff, then a lighter shade, and after that the lightest color. This color sequence is then repeated once more. The Icelandic lace weight has approx. 229 m (250 yd)/50 g.

Needles: 2 and 2.5 mm (US 0 and 2) double pointed needles.

Cast on 56 stitches with 2 mm (US 0) double pointed needles and divide the stitches evenly on to 4 needles; 14 stitches on each needle. Join to knit in the round and work 2x2 rib (knit 2, purl 2) for 8 cm/3 inches. Change to 2.5 mm (US 2) needles, knit 1 row and increase 10 stitches evenly spread throughout the row, 66 sts. Now change to a lighter shade of the yarn and start to knit the lace pattern as follows: *Row 1:* [knit 1, yarn over, knit 3 stitches. Slip 1 stitch knitwise, knit 1, pass slipped stitch over the knit one, knit 2 together. Knit 3 stitches, yarn over], repeat to end of row. *Row 2:* knit. Repeat these two rows throughout the mitten. I like to knit 12 rows with each color. Knit until the mitten measures 6 cm/2½ inches from the cuff (for me, this is usually after 12 rows with one color and antoher 12 rows with a different color), then it's time to make the thumb opening. **Right mitten:** knit 2 stitches from needle 1, then knit the next 11 stitches on to scrap yarn for the thumb. Move the 11 stitches back to the left needle and knit them again with the main color. Knit to end of row. **Left mitten:** knit untill 13 stitches are left on needle 4, knit the next 11 stitches on a scrap yarn. Move the 11 stitches back to the left needle and knit them again with the main color. Knit the 2 remaining stitches of the row. Now knit 3 x 12 rows with different colors as described earlier (if you are in fact knitting your mittens with three different colors). When the mitten measures 17 cm/6½ inches from the cuff, begin decreasing for the top. The rest of the mitten is knit in plain stockinette stitch, not the lace pattern. **Decreases:** *needle 1:* knit. [*Needle 2:* knit untill 1 stitch is left on the needle, slip it knitwise. *Needle 3:* knit 2 stitches together, pass the slipped stitch from needle 2 over the new stitch, knit to end of needle. *Needle 4:* knit untill 1 stitch is left on needle, slip it knitwise. Needle 1: knit 2 together, pass slipped stitch from needle 4 over the new stitch]. Repeat from [to] for every row of the mitten until 3 stitches remain on each needle. Break yarn and pull through the remaining stitches. **Thumb:** remove the scrap yarn from the 11 thumb stitches, this leaves a hole in your work. Pick upp 11 stitches above the hole, and 11 stitches below the hole, and 1-2 stitches on each side of the hole as well. It's better to pick up more stitches than fewer along the sides, as this will prevent holes at the base of the thumb. Extra stitches can always be decreased in the first rounds of the thumb by knitting 2 together on the sides of the thumb. The total number of thumbstitches should be 24. Divide these stitches evenly between 3 needles and work stockinette stitch in the round for 5.5 – 6 cm/2¼ inches. Now decrease for the top of the thumb like this: [knit 1, knit 2 together], repeat to end of row. Knit 1 row. Next row: [knit 2 together], repeat to end of row. Break yarn and pull through the remaining stitches. Knit the other mitten. Weave in all loose ends, wash the mittens in luke warm water with a drop of wool soap. You can give them a little rub while they're in the water if you want to felt them a bit. Lay to dry.

Every knitter knows how bags and boxes become easily filled with yarn and yarn leftovers. Kristrún has experienced this, and so she made an honest attempt to destash. She decided to knit a pair of mittens every week for one whole year. She succeeded, and one year later her great grandmother's old treasturechest was halffull with 52 unique and beautiful pairs of mittens.

Jóhanna

Jóhanna Hjaltadóttir, a 90 year old from Reykjavík, is a true gem among knitters. Visiting her is like entering a knitted wonderland, as almost everything in her house is knitted or decorated with knitting! It seems like Jóhanna has knit the whole world. Jóhanna is very creative, and her creativity knows no bounds when it comes to knitting: "What I like best is to improvise without a pattern and see how it turns out", she says. Jóhanna has knit everything from dresses, shawls, sweaters and blankets, to more unusual items such as lampshades and bathing suits! Despite her advanced years she still enjoys knitting, mostly for her grandchildren and her great grandchildren who regularly place orders for what kind of knitwear they would like. She also enjoys knitting pairs of the slippers she presents to you here, and usually has them on her needles when she has no other projects lined up.

Knitting motto: *I'm not afraid to frog if I know it will improve my knitting*

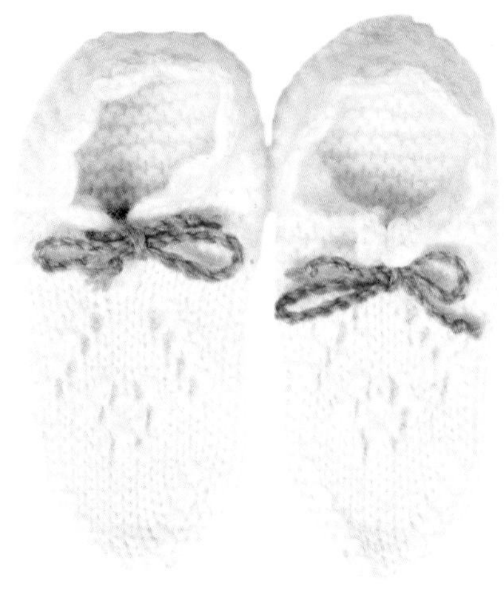

Princess Slippers

Jóhanna´s slippers are since long well known, she was probably the first person to knit this type of slipper here in Iceland. "I really didn´t like to knit ribbing, which is the main reason why I designed these rib-free ankle socks. And they soon became very popular" she says, and no wonder as these are convenient and clever little anklets. She tends to knit them when she has nothing else to knit, and she knows their lace pattern by heart, luckily, as her eyesight is getting worse. She always has a few pairs ready in her treasure chest. Her girlfriends use them as sleeping socks – and sometimes she does too.

Size: ladies size medium.
Yarn: 2 strands Icelandic unspun wool, or other yarn of similar weight that gives you same gauge.
Needles: 4.5 mm (US 7) double pointed needles.
Gauge: 18 stitches in garter stitch make 10 cm/4inches

Cast on 30 stitches, and knit garter stitch back and forth for 24 rows. Now join to work in the round and divide the stitches on to 3 needles, like this: 7 first and 8 last stitches on to the first needle, 7 stitches on to the second needle, and 8 stitches on to the third needle. Knit in the round and the work lace pattern from the **chart** on the instep on needle 1 for a total of 14 rounds. After that, begin decreasing for the toe. **Decreases:** round 1: needle 1: knit 1, slip 1, knit 1, pass the slipped stitch over the knit one. Knit to last 3 stitches, knit 2 together, knit 1. Needle 2: knit 1, slip 1, knit 1, pass the slipped stitch over the knit one. Knit to end of needle. Third needle: knit to last 3 stitches, knit 2 together, knit 1. Round 2: knit. Repeat rounds 1 and 2 until 10 stitches remain. Cut yarn and graft the 10 stitches together with the Kitchener stitch. Sew the heel together, weave in all ends. Knit the other slipper.

Jóhanna sometimes crochets around the opening on her slippers – and when she does so she calls them ***princess slippers.*** *She crochets "flower petals" around the* opening, or something like this: work 1 single crochet, chain 1, 2 double crochets in the same hole/stitch on the edge (flower petal made), skip 2 ridges, work next flower petal in next ridge. Repeat this all around the opening.

Note: *the crochet terminology used in this pattern is in American English, see page 29 for British crochet terms.*

Ties for the slippers: fold 90 cm/35 inches long string of Lopi lite or other worsted yarn and twist together. Repeat this to make another string, and then twist these two together to make a tie about 40 cm/16 inches long. Thread the tie from the front around the opening of the slipper in the "holes" along the edges. Make another tie for the second slipper.

Lace pattern for slippers

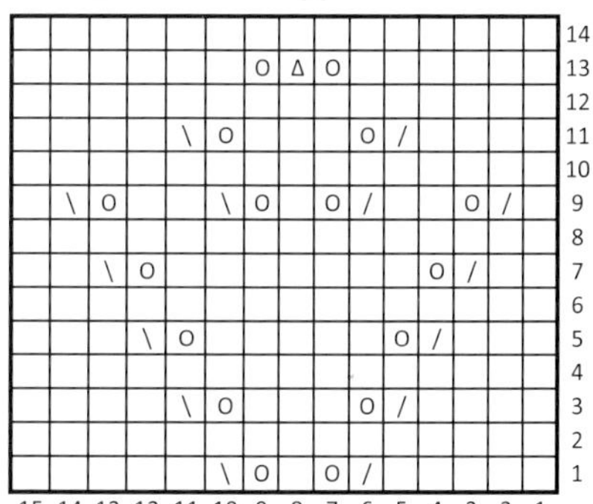

☐ = Knit

/ = Knit 2 together

\ = Slip 1, knit 1, pass the slipped stitch over the knit one

O = Yarn over

Δ = Slip 1, slip 1, knit 1, pass both slipped stitches over the knit one

Perla

Make your own knitting mottos!

Our Knitting Mottos!

1. The success of your knitting depends to a great extent on your choice of yarn and colors. Simple, plain projects can be made great with the "right" yarn in the "right" colors.
2. Knit joy and happiness into every stitch!
3. Relax and have fun while knitting – that's usually the point of the whole thing anyways.
4. When it comes to knitting, all mistakes are fixable.
5. Swatch! Take a little time to test your gauge – it might save you a LOT of time later.
6. Add personal touches to every little project to make it your own.
7. Handknits are a joy to both give and receive.
8. Never stop experimenting with your knitting. Try out a new method in your next project.
9. Spread the joy, and teach someone to knit or crochet :-)
10. Knit a few rows every day.

Helga

Helga Linnet is a 35 year old draftsman from Hafnarfjörður in the South of Iceland, and a mother of three. She remembers clearly that when she was younger she wanted to learn how to knit, but didn't feel confident enough to try it since she's left-handed. It wasn't until she´d carefully studied her grandmother's knitting techniques that Helga finally borrowed some yarn and needles, snuck into her room and knit her very first item: a doll's sweater. She worked out her own methods of assembling knitted garments, making up her own patterns as she went along and soon her dolls had wardrobes full of clothes. So you could say that she began her career as a knitwear designer early in life. She says she still doesn't like to follow knitting patterns, but she often uses them as a guide or a source of inspiration. When she was sixteen, she'd already knit several baby dresses and blankets, and around twenty she had designed so many things that even older and more experienced knitters began contacting her for advice. Helga always keeps her knitting close to hand and knits at any occasion. She can knit and cook at the same time, and recently bought a robot vacuum cleaner so she can minimize the time spent on house-cleaning and spend more time on the important stuff, namely KNITTING!

Knitting motto: *A few rows a day make my day*

Lopi Gloves

Great gloves, perfect for "him". Knit this set, and he won't have an excuse for not wearing a matching hat and gloves... :-)

Size: man's size medium or woman's size large. The length of the fingers is easily adjustable.
Yarn: Lopi lite, gray 50g and beige, 20 g., or other yarn of a similar weight that gives you the same gauge. Lopi lite is a worsted/light worsted yarn, and has approx. 100 m (109 yd)/50 g.
Needles: 3.5 and 4 mm (US 5 and 6) double pointed needles. Adjust needle size if necessary to obtain the correct gauge.
Gauge: 18 stitches in stockinette stitch with 4 mm needles (US 6) = 10 cm/4 inches.

Cast on 36 stitches on 3.5 mm (US 5) needles, join to knit in the round and work 1x1 ribbing (knit 1, purl 1) for 5 cm/2 inches. Change to 4 mm (US 6) needles, and work in stockinette stitch. Increase 10 stitches evenly spaced in the first row. Knit 10 rows. Now begin increasing for the thumb. A good way to make the increases is to knit into the stitch below the next stitch on the left needle. **Thumb-increases for the right glove:** row 1: knit 1, increase 1, knit, 1 increase 1, knit to end of row. Row 2: knit. Row 3: knit 1, increase 1, knit 3, increase 1, knit to end of row. Row 4: knit. Row 5: knit 1, increase 1, knit 5, increase 1, knit to end of row. Row 6: place the first 8 stitches (thumb stitches) on a stitch holder. Cast on 4 stitches above the thumb stitches and join with the rest of the glove for a total of 48 stitches. **Thumb-increases for the left glove:** row 1: knit until 2 stitches remain of row, place marker. Knit 1, increase 1, knit, 1 increase 1. Row 2: knit. Row 3: knit to marker, knit 1, increase 1, knit 3, increase 1. Row 4: knit. Row 5: knit to marker, knit 1, increase 1, knit 5, increase 1. Row 6: Place the last 8 stitches (thumb stitches) on a stitch holder. Cast on 4 stitches above the thumb stitches and join with the rest of the glove You should now have a total of 48 stitches. Knit 2 rows, then knit the pattern from the chart. When you're done with the pattern, it's time to knit the fingers. Place all stitches on 2 needles, 24 stitches on each needle. The thumb should be placed exactly on the side of the mitten, between the two needles. **Middle finger:** divide the next 6 stitches from each needle evenly over 3 needles (12 sts). Join to knit in the round and work stockinette stitch until the finger measures 9 cm/3½ inhces. Knit 2 and 2 together throughout the next round. Break yarn and pull through the remaining 6 stitches. **Ring finger:** divide the next 6 stitches from each needle evenly over 3 needles (12 sts). Join to knit in the round and work stockinette stitch until the finger measures 8 cm/3 inches. Knit 2 and 2 together throughout the next round. Break yarn and pull through the remaining 6 stitches. **Little finger:** divide the next 6 stitches from each needle evenly over 3 needles. Join to knit in the round and work stockinette stitch until the finger measures 7 cm/2¾. Knit 2 and 2 together throughout the next round. Break yarn and pull through the remaining 6 stitches. **Index finger:** divide the first 6 stitches from each needle evenly over 3 needles (12 sts). Join to knit in the round and work stockinette stitch until the finger measures 8 cm/3 inches. Knit 2 and 2 together throughout the next round. Break yarn and pull through the remaining 6 stitches. **Thumb:** pick up the 8 thumb stitches, pick up 4 stitches from the cast on above the thumb, and also pick up 2 stitches on each side of the thumb = 16 stitches. Divide the stitches evenly on 3 needles, join to knit in the round. Knit 4-5 cm/1½ - 2 inches. Now knit 2 and 2 together throughout the next round. Break yarn and pull through the remainin stitches. Weave in all loose ends. Knit the other glove!

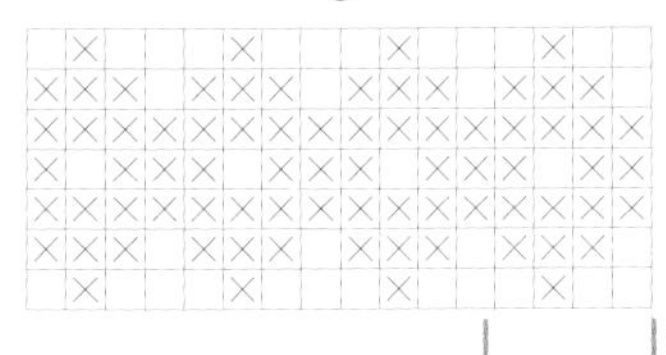

Repeat this pattern

Lopi Hat

Size: medium. It's very easy to adjust the size of the hat by increasing or decreasing the number of stitches cast on. Just remember that the pattern repeat is 4 stitches, so the number of cast on stitches has to be divisible by 4.
Yarn: same as for the gloves, Lopi lite, gray 50 g and beige, 20 g.
Needles: 4 mm (US 6) circular needles, 40 cm/16 inches long, and double pointed needles.
Gauge: 18 stitches in stockinette stitch = 10 cm/4 inches.

Cast on 88 stitches on 4 mm (US 6) circular needles. Join to knit in the round and knit 11 rows. Purl 1 row. Knit 5 rows, and then knit the pattern from the chart. Knit for 17-20 cm/7-8 inches, depending on how long you want the hat to be. On the next row, knit 2 and 2 together throughout. Break yarn and pull through the remaning stitches. Fold the hat where the purled row is, and fasten the edge down. Weave in all ends.

Erla Sigurlaug

Erla is a 33 year old social anthropologist who becomes consumed with ambition when she gets an idea into her head. Like knitting. And publishing a knitting book but she's one of the authors of this book. She learned how to knit when she was a child but was too impatient for the knitting to take hold at that point. All the women in her family are obsessed with knitting and they were quite astounded that Erla didn´t like to knit as much as they did. Until last year. Then something happened. Erla finally grew up, gained some patience, grabbed her knitting needles, and now she can´t stop! Her favorite projects are quick and cute little things she likes to improvise and design herself, although she occasionally also has bigger challenges on her needles. To Erla, most knitting patterns look like Chinese, so she's invested her energy more into making up her own patterns, and just seeing what happens, like a total adrenaline junkie! And of course she calls her mom or cousin Halldóra for HELP when everything turns into a big mess...!

Knitting motto: *Knitting eases my mind and stops me from being restless all the time. It teaches me patience, so I never want to stop...*

Scarf Goes Through

This scarf is really comfortable because you don´t have to tie it; just pull one end through the hole! You can easily decorate the scarf as you wish. You can for example crochet with single crochets around the edges with different colored yarn, or make flowers and fasten them on. The scarf looks good on both kids and grown ups (I sometimes borrow it from my daughter...!)

Yarn: Mohair, color bright pink and Katia Brisa 27, color golden (or some other shiny cotton viscose yarn) held and knit together, 1 skein of each.
Needles: 8 mm (US 11) long needles or circular needle and a 3 mm (US D) crochet hook.
Gauge: 11 stitches in garter stitch with the recommended yarn and needles should be 10 cm/4 inches.
Note: *the crochet terminology used in this pattern is in American English, see page 29 for British crochet terms.*

Loosely cast on 14 stitches using 8mm (US 11) needles. Knit garter stitch back and forth for 26 rows or until the scarf measures about 16 cm/6½ inches. Then it's time make the hole. You divide the stitches in half by putting every other stitch on to a stitch holder or spare needle (7 stitches) and leaving them until later. Knit 8 rows in garter stitch with the 7 stitches left on the needle, then put them on a spare needle/holder. Now knit the other 7 stitches in the same way. After that,

Vera wearing her pink scarf

combine the 14 stitches again on to one needle by knitting 1 stitch alternately from the needle and spare needle/holder. Now continue knitting 40 – 44 rows of garter stitch, or around 28 -30 cm/11-12 inches. Then it's time to begin decreasing (for the part of the scarf that goes through the hole.) On the next row, knit two together to the end of the row, leaving 7 stitches on the needle. Knit 6 rows garter stitch with these 7 stitches. Now increase again by knitting into the front and back of every stitch so there are 14 stitches again on your needle. Knit garter stitch for 26 rows or about 16 cm/6½ inches, just like on the other end of the scarf. **Decorating** the scarf is fun; here we've worked single crochet around one end of the scarf and attached little flowers on the other end.

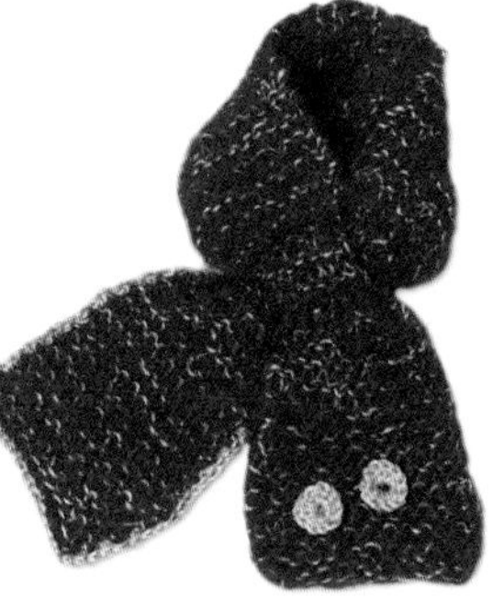

Perla

"Properly practiced, knitting soothes the troubled spirit and it doesn´t hurt the untroubled spirit either."
Elizabeth Zimmermann
knitting guru
1910 - 1999

The easiest flower ever: crochet hook size 3 (US D) and golden yarn. Chain 3 and join with a slip stitch in to a circle. Work double crochets in the circle – as many as you possibly can – and when there is no more room for double crochets, join the last one with the first one you made with a slip stitch, and voila – you have the cutest little flower for your scarf :-)

Garter Stich Bib

This one is great for drooling infants and messy dinner times! It takes only two hours to knit.

Yarn: Mandarin petit, cotton yarn, 1 skein, or other cotton yarn of similar weight.
Needles: 3.5mm (US 4) round needle or a long needle.
Gauge: 21 stitches in garter stitch should be 10 cm/4 inches.
Other: 1 button.

Cast on 45 stitches. Knit garter stitch until the bib is around 18 cm/ 7 inches long. Cast off 31 stitches and continue to knit the other 14 stitches; these stitches form the bib's neckband. Knit the **neckband** until it's around 22 cm/9 inches long. Then make a **buttonhole** in the middle of neckband: knit 5 stitches, cast off 2-3 stitches (depends on how big a button you will be using), knit 6 stitches. On the next round, knit 6 stitches, make 3 stitches with the backward loop cast on (as shown in the photo) and knit 5 stitches. Knit 2 cm/1 inch from the buttonhole, then bind off. Altogether the neckband is around 25 cm/10 inches long. Sew a button on to the bib.

Erla Sigurlaug

Free-style Necklaces

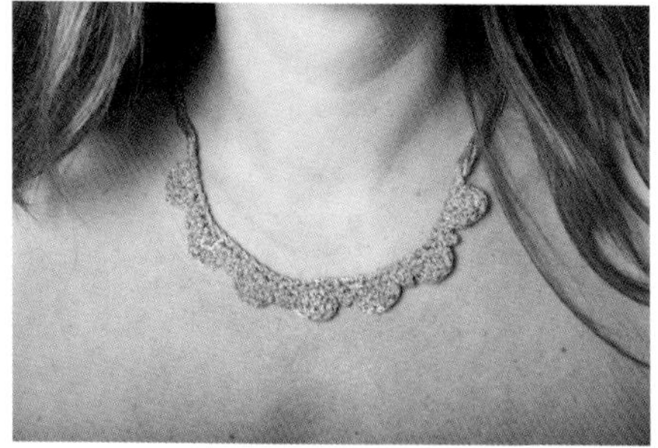

Goldie Locks

The Rock Princess

Snow White

These necklaces are meant to be an inspiration for others to design and crochet their own necklace. Here you're provided with two patterns, but you should definitively free your inner necklace design goddess and see what happens. Free-style is the keyword here!

The method is simple. Start by making a chain. Then you can for example: **A)** Crochet a "flower petal" on to the chain like in the **Goldie Lock**s neclace. The petals are made of single crochets, double crochets and treble crochets worked in one and the same stitch. The size of the petals depends on how many you do of each. **B)** Crochet "shells" by making a chain arch, and in the next round filling the chain arch with double crochets, like in the necklace **Snow White**. **C)** Alternate flower petals and shells, with a space inbetween, or perhaps not... and so on. You can use yarn in any color you like, even mixing colors together, and you can decorate the necklace with beads or whatever you like.

Goldie Locks

Yarn: golden crochet yarn, for example Glamour from Hjertegarn or Four Seasons.
Crochet hook: Size 2.5 – 3 mm (US B-D)
Other: a necklace clasp for the necklace, and fabric stiffener ("Stiffy" for example) to stiffen the fabric. Available in craft shops.
Abbreviations: st = stitch, sc = single crochet, dc = double crochet, tc = triple crochet.
Note: *this pattern uses American English crochet terminology, see page 29 for British crochet terms.*

Chain 37, loosely. Work single crochets (sc) in the chain, 1 in each stitch (st), turn. Work sc in the first st. Now make flower petals and a small picot stitch in between them across the row. Each flower petal and picot stitch are worked into 5 stitches. *Flower petal*: *sc in next st, 1 sc, 1 dc, 1 tc in next st, 1 tc, 1 dc, 1 sc in next st, 1 sc in next st, slip stitch in next st. **Picot stitch:** chain 3, join with a slip stitch to 4th st from hook. Now repeat from * and make alternating flower petals and picot stitches until you have 7 flower petals and 6 picot stitches. Finish the row by making one single crochet in the last stitch. Now the necklace itself is ready, make the "chain". There are many ways to make the chain, but here it's made with several strands of yarn. The chain on one side: Thread a long length of the yarn through the last single crochet 4 times very loosely, so the threads are the length you want the chain to be – try it on! Now you have 8 threads, make sure they are equally long. Take a short piece of yarn and wrap it around the end of the chain right by the last flower petal and tie a knot. Also make a knot at the other end of the chain where the lock will be fastened. You can cut the threads close to the knot, because the fabric stiffener will make them stiff and prevent them from unraveling. The necklace has a tendency to twist a bit which is why fabric stiffener is a good idea. Brush some fabric stiffener on to the necklace but not on the chain (the yarn in the chain should stay soft) and let it dry. Sew a clasp on to the chain and enjoy wearing this simple homemade glamour item around your neck.

The Rock Princess

Yarn: cotton crochet yarn, like Solberg 12/4 (for 2-2.5 mm crochet hook, US B-C) or regular cotton yarn like Mandarin Classic (for 3 mm crochet hook, US C-D), or similar yarn.
Crochet hook: size 2-3 mm (US B-D).
Other: a metal necklace chain and a clasp, and fabric stiffener ("Stiffy" for example) to stiffen the fabric. Available in most craft shops.
Abbreviations: st = stitch, sc = single crochet, dc = double crochet, tc = treble crochet.
Note: *this pattern uses American English crochet terminology, see page 29 for British crochet terms.*

You can either crochet the necklace directly on to a metal necklace chain, or you can crochet the lacy necklace and then fasten a metal necklace chain to each side of it – which I actually find easier. Here hovewer I show you how to crochet the necklace directly on to a metal chain, like shown on the photo.
Row 1: work 41 single crochets (sc) around the metal necklace chain, and make sure that the stitches are even and not twisted on the chain. The metal chain should be equally long on both sides of the 41 single crochets, so the necklace clasp will be placed in the center of the back of your neck. Turn. *Row 2:* 1 sc in each of next 3 stitches (sts), 1 double crochet (dc) in next st. Now work [3 treble crochets (tc) in next st, chain 2, skip next 2 sts], repeat until you have made 10 2-chain spaces, and 5 sts are left. Work 3 tc in next st, and end like you began the row: 1 dc in next st, and 1 sc in each of next 3 sts, turn. *Row 3:* work sc in every st until you get to the first 2-chain space. Work 6 tc in each of next four 2-chain spaces = a total of 24 tc. Now work 4 tc in each of next two 2-chain space (this is the center of the necklace) = 8 tc, and then 6 tc in each of next four 2-chain space again = 24 tc. Now work sc to the end of the row, turn. *Row 4:* work sc until you get to the middle of the first 6-tc group. Now make "*tops*" in the middle of the 6-tc groups, like this: *[work 1 sc, 2 dc, 1 sc in the space between the 3rd and 4th tc of the next 6-tc group, slip st in the last tc of the 6-tc group (full top made). Chain 6 and join with a slip st in the first tc of the next 6-tc group (open top made)], repeat from [to] altogether 3 times, so you have a total of 6 tops – 3 full and 3 open. Now make 1 more full top in the space between the 3rd and 4th tc of the next 6-tc group: 1 sc, 2 dc, 1 sc, join with a slip st in the last tc in the 6-tc group. Chain 9 and join with a slip st into the space between 2nd and 3rd tc in next 4-tc-group. Chain 11, join with a slip st into the space between 2nd and 3rd tc in next 4-tc-group (this is the middle of the necklace). Chain 9 again and join with a slip st in first tc in the next 6-tc group. Now make tops the same way you did on the other side, alternating 4 full and 3 empty tops, work from *. Sc in every stitch to end of row. Break yarn. *Row 5:* now make 5 loops in the middle of the necklace, like this: Start crocheting just before the last "full top" before the middle, join in the slip st between top no. 6 and 7. Chain 9, join with a slip st in next slip st from previous row (after top no. 7). Chain 11, join with a slip st in next slip st from previous row. Chain 15, join with a slip st in next slip st from previous row (this is the center of the necklace). Chain 11 again, and join with a slip st in next slip st from previous row. Finally, chain 9 and join with a slip st in next slip st from previous row. Break yarn.

Finishing: weave in all loose ends. Wet with a fabric stiffener. I usually dilute it with a little bit of water (to prevent it from getting too stiff). Shape your nice little lacy necklace so it will look good on your neck (not too tight and not to open) and lay to dry. When dry, fasten a clasp on the necklace, and, at the next party you go to, wear your gorgeous necklace and rock´n roll like a **Rock Princess!**

Erla Sigurlaug

Happy Hat with a Tassel

"My 5 year old daughter wanted a hat with a tassel, and this hat is the result of my subsequent experiments with the crochet hook. The hat is warm, doesn't itch and I think it makes every little girl look cute and happy. You can't help but be happy wearing a hat like that.... :-)"

Size: 4-6 year old, or to fit a head circumference around 50-52 cm/20 inches (medium adult size, or to fit head circumference around 57 cm/22½ inches). It's advisable to measure the chain you begin with against the head of the future owner of the hat. It's actually very easy to make this hat in any size you want...
Yarn: Eskimo wool yarn from Drops, 2 skeins multi color, and 1 skein in white, or other bulky yarn. Silver or gold shiny crochet yarn for the flower, for example Glamour from Hjertegarn.
Crochet hook: 7 mm (US K-L) for the hat itself and 4-5 mm (US G-H) for the shiny crochet yarn to decorate the flower.
Note: *this pattern uses crochet terminology American English crochet terminology, see page 29 for British crochet terms.*

Chain 54 (60) with the multi colored yarn, or chain until the chain fits around the head of its future owner. Join into a circle with a slip stitch. *Round 1:* work single crochets (sc) in every stitch (st). *Row 2:* *Sc in each of the next 5 st, skip next stitch, repeat from * - 45 (50) sts. Work sc in every st around for 8 (10) rounds, or more depending on what fits the head of the intended recipient. Now start to decrease. **Decrease:** work sc in every st, but skip every 9th st around - 40 (45) st. Next row: work sc in every st, but skip every 8th st around. Next row: 1 sc in each st around. Continue like this until you have only 1 st left, break yarn. The shape of the top of the hat depends on how often or seldom you decrease. You can easily change the look of your hat by improvising; skipping fewer or more loops and working more rounds without decreases in between. Don't be afraid to experiment!

Now, the tassel: use white yarn, or any other color than the hat itself. Make two chains of 10 st. Leave a thread on both ends of the chains. Make a tassel by cutting yarn into even 8 cm/ 3 inches lengths, tie a knot in their middle with the thread from one end of both of the chains you made, so the tassel is now joined with the chains. Tie another thread around the tassel to make the tiny bulb on top of the tassel. Sew the tassel on to the top of the hat. For decoration, you can wrap decorative crochet yarn around the chains close to the tassel.

Crochet on the edge of the hat: *row 1:* Work sc in every st, but skip every 9th (10th) st. If the hat is already is a tight fit and you don't want it to get any smaller, work sc in every st. Next row: make small flower petals: *work 1 sc, 1 dc (double crochet), 1 sc in next st. Chain 2, skip 2 st, repeat from * around. For the bigger size of the hat skip 3 st instead of 2 for the flower petals to match the round.

The flower: you can make any kind of flower to decorate the hat. This flower is made of three different sized flowers sewn together. *The biggest flower:* chain 5, join with a slip st in to a circle. Next row: Make 6 petals by chaining 10, join in to the ring with a slip st, repeat 5 more times. *The middle flower:* like the biggest flower but smaller, chain 6 instead of 10. To decorate, use another color of yarn (the shiny gold or silver colored crochet yarn, for example) and 4-5 mm crochet hook (US G-H). Work sc in each st of the flower petals on the big and the middle flower. *The smallest flower:* chain 3, join with a slip st in to a circle. *Row 1:* work as many dc as possibly fit into the ring. Now sew the three flowers together and fasten a bead in the middle. Sew the flower on to the hat, put it on the head of its new owner and he or she will always have **fun** wearing it!

Vera having fun with her hats

Cozy Ribbed Hat

"I made this hat when I realized that I didn't have a warm, cosy hat, but a huge stash of Icelandic unspun wool and Einband, the Icelandic laceweight. This hat is unbelievably warm and looks great on any head. And best of all, it can be knit in only two hours!"

Size: adults and kids – the rib is stretchy and fits all, just knit a longer hat for bigger heads.
Yarn: 4 strands Icelandic unspun wool and one strand of a different color of Einband, Icelandic laceweight, all held together. You need about 70 g for each hat.
Needles: 10 mm (US 15) circular needles, 40 cm/16 inches long.

Loosely cast on 30 stitches, or 32 stitches for a bigger size (for a large head). It is very important that the cast on is loose. Knit 1 stitch through the back loop and purl 1 until the hat is around 28 cm/11 inches long for adults and 24 cm/9½ inches long for kids, or as long as you want it to be. Knitting into the back loop of the stitch twists the stitch and makes it stand out a bit, which gives definition to the rib. The hat should be long but not too slouchy. Break the yarn, leaving a short tail, and pull through all of the stitches. Be careful when you pull the yarn through – the Icelandic unspun wool is fragile. For extra cuteness, attach a pom-pom to the top of the hat.

Erla Sigurlaug

TV Socks

- Golden oldies

"Knit woolen socks without having to make a heel or using 5 needles! The TV-Socks are totally comfortable, both to knit and to wear. This is a traditional Icelandic pattern, copied from old socks I have that my grandmother knit for me a long time ago. The pattern is really simple; the socks are just knit back and forth with no heel to complicate things. If you want cozy and warm socks for lounging in, then these TV-Socks are just the thing. These socks are for relaxing, watching TV – and knitting, of course!"

Size: medium adult size (one size fits all), length: 48 – 50 cm/19-20 inches. Children's size (2-5 year old), length: 30 cm/12 inches.
Yarn: adult size: Álafoss Lopi, or 2 strands Icelandic Unspun wool, in 4 colors. You need a total of 170 g (Álafoss lopi has approx. 100 m (109 yd.)/100 g). Children's size: Lopi lite, in 4 colors of your choice , you need a total of 70 g for a pair of socks. (Lopi lite has approx. 100 m (109 yd)/50 g.
Needles: adult size: 6 mm (US 10) long needles or circular needles. Children's size: 4.5 mm (US 7) long needles or circular needles.
Gauge: *adult size:* 11 stitches in garter stitch with Álafoss Lopi should be 10 cm/4 inches. *Children's size:* 15 stitches in garter stitch with Lopi lite should be 10 cm/4 inches.

These socks are knit back and forth lengthwise. You start knitting at the front of the sock in the middle of the stockinette stitch part. Increases are worked from the toes. When you change colors, do it when knitting on the right side, so color changes only show on the wrong side. Choose your favorite colors for this fun project!
Cast on 45 stitches. Cast on more stitches if you want the sock to be longer than about 48 cm/19 inches (30 cm/12 inches).
The stockinette stitch part on the front of the sock: adult and children´s sizes:
Row 1: purl across.
Row 2: increase 1 stitch in the beginning of the row (by the toe), knit across.
Row 3: purl across.
Row 4: increase 1 stitch in the beginning of the row, knit across.
Row 5: purl across.
Children's size: stop working the stockinette stitch part and move over to the garter stitch part.
Adult size, continue with *Row 6:* increase 1 stitch in the beginning of the row, knit across.
Row 7: purl across.

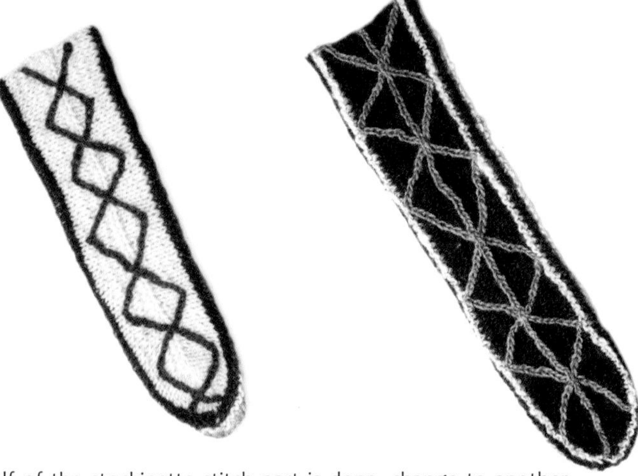
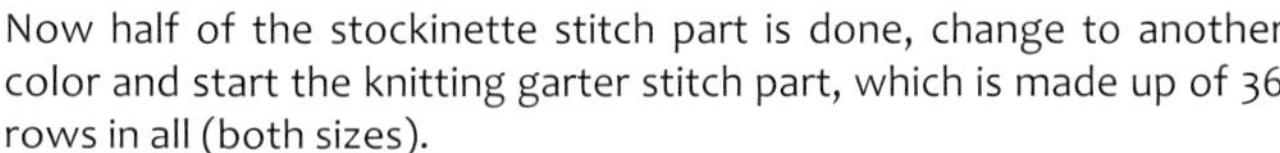

Now half of the stockinette stitch part is done, change to another color and start the knitting garter stitch part, which is made up of 36 rows in all (both sizes).

The garter stitch part:

Rows 1 – 6: knit back and forth, use different colors, but knit each two rows with the same color.

Rows 7 – 30: knit garter stitch with yet another color (this is the back of the sock) .

Rows 31-32: knit with the same color as in garter stitch rows 5-6.

Rows 33-34: knit with the same color as in garter stitch rows 3-4.

Rows 35-36: knit with the same color as in garter stitch rows 1-2.

Now you have completed the garter stitch part, 36 rows altogether. Change to the same color you started knitting the sock with and work the other half of the stockinette stitch part for the front of the sock.

The other half of the stockinette stitch part in the front:

Row 1 (Right side): with the same color used in the other half of the stockinette stitch part, knit across.

Row 2: purl across.

Row 3: decrease by knitting 2 stitches together at the beginning of the row, knit until end of row.

Row 4: purl across.

Row 5: knit 2 together at the beginning of the row, knit until end of row.

Row 6: purl across.

Children's size: now it's time to cast off if you're knitting the children´s size. Adult size, continue with *Row 7:* knit 2 together at the beginning of the row, knit until end of row.

Row 8: purl across.

Row 9: cast off.

Finishing: weave in all loose ends. Sew the sock together from the right side (except the toe part), by making the cast on and cast off edges meet (put the needle in the middle of the cast off stitches on the edge). Sew the toe from the wrong side, and try to make it look even on the right side. Break the yarn. Using a yarn needle, thread through those last stitches to form the toe, and pull them together. Embellish the socks with an embroidered or crocheted pattern. Knit the other TV sock. Now put your socks on your cold feet and enjoy relaxing – in front of the **TV** of course!

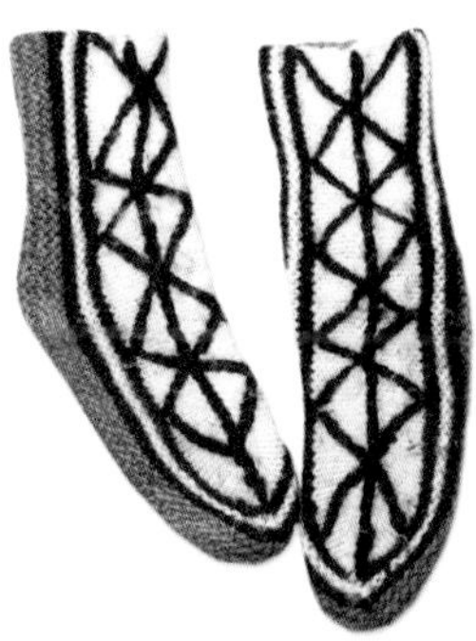

Erla´s TV socks that her late grandma Sigurlaug knit for her many years ago.

When TV broadcasting first began in Iceland in 1966 it soon became the center of the attention in people's homes. Playing cards lost its popularity and people stopped reading books as much as they used to. The director of the national television broadcaster demanded that everyone who appeared on TV watch their language and speak in a respectable manner because being on TV was seen as a very serious and ceremonial event, as was broadcasting and even watching TV. A new culture soon evolved around this technological wonder. People ate special TV snacks on TV nights, everyone had their own TV cup to drink from as they watched, and each home had a special TV blanket. The housewives even knit special TV socks (the pattern presented here) that the whole family was supposed to wear while watching TV, to prevent their feet from getting cold while sitting still.

Erla Sigurlaug

Start knitting the pattern here – unless you want to have the Space Invader upside down on the mitten, in which case you start in the bottom right corner.

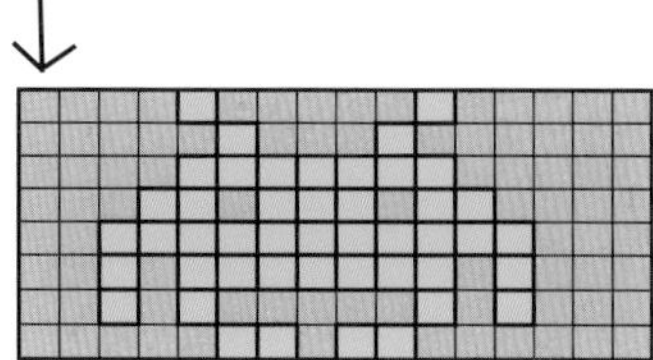

Space Mittens

"I made these mittens especially for my girlfriend and gave her for her birthday. She likes things that are a bit "different", like the classic videogame Space Invaders. She couldn't believe her own eyes when she unwrapped the present and was delighted with this personal gift made especially made her." Why not make these mittens for your friends, or design your own pattern to decorate them with. Surprise your friends and give them a personal gift!

Size: medium. Length: 25 cm/10 inches, width: 10.5 cm/ 4 inches. You get bigger mittens by using a 3 strands of the Icelandic unspun and larger needles, or 5 and 6 mm (8 and 10) needles.
Yarn: 2 strands Icelandic unspun wool, gray, white and green, or the colors you like, about 60 g. The Icelandic unspun has approx. 300 m (328 yd)/100 g.
Needles: 4.5 mm and 5.5 mm (US 7 and 9) double pointed needles.
Gauge: 15 stitches in stockinette stitch with 5.5 mm (US 9) needles should be 10 cm/4 inches.

Cast on 32 stitches with white yarn using 4.5 mm (US 7) needles. Divide the stitches evenly on four needles and join to knit in the round. Work *seed/moss stitch** for the first 4 rounds. Now switch to 5.5 mm (US 9) needles and knit stockinette stitch. Knit two rounds with green, one with gray and again one with green. From now on knit only with gray. When the mitten measures about 11-12 cm/4½ inches long, make the opening for the thumb. **Right mitten:** knit the first stitch on the first needle, then knit the next 7 stitches on to scrap yarn for the thumb opening. Move them back on to left needle and knit them again with the main color. Knit to the end of the row. **Left mitten:** knit until 8 stitches are left on needle 4, knit the next 7 stitches on to scrap yarn for the thumb opening. Move the 7 scrap yarn stitches back on to left needle and knit them again with the main color. Knit the last stitch on the needle. Now start knitting the **Space Invader pattern** on back of the hand, see chart. Since there is no pattern in the palm of the hand, pull the green yarn back behind the Space Invader pattern to be worked in the next pattern row, being careful not to pull to tigthly. Twist the gray and the green strands together when you pull the green back to prevent holes. When the pattern is done, knit until the mitten measures around 13 cm/5 inches from the thumb (size medium, longer for larger mittens). Now begin decreasing for the top of the mitten. **Decrease row:** *first needle:* slip 1, knit 1, pass the slipped stitch over the knit one (skp), knit to end of needle. *Second needle:* knit until 2 stitches are left on the needle, knit 2 together. *Third needle:* same as first needle. *Fourth needle:* same as second needle. Repeat these decreases every row until 8 stitches remain, two on each needle. Break yarn and pull through the remaining stitches. **Thumb:** remove the scrap yarn from the 7 stitches, and pick up stitches to knit the thumb (with 5.5 mm (US 9) needles). Pick up 7 stitches below the opening, 8 above the opening, and 1 beside the opening = 16 stitches. Put 8 stitches on one needle and divide the others on two needles. Knit 15 rounds (or more if you want longer thumb). Now start decreasing like you decreased for the top of the mitten, by knitting a skp for a left leaning decrease, and knitting 2 together for a right leaning decrease. 4 sts are decreased like this per row for the next two rows, leaving 8 stitches. Break yarn and pull through the remaining stitches. Weave in all ends. Carefully weave over the Space Invader picture from the wrong side so your fingers won´t get stuck in the threads. Knit the other mitten!

**Seed/moss stitch: knit 1, purl 1, and on the next row do the opposite: purl 1 on top of a knit stitch, knit 1 on top of a purl stitch.*

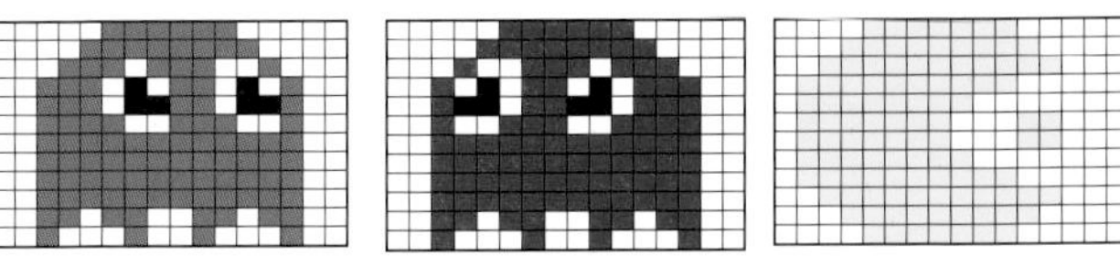

Here you have some patterns to put on your mitten

Brioche!

The brioche stitch is easier than it first appears - I promise! I just recently learned how to do it; I simply followed the instructions and it worked out perfectly for me, even though I'm a beginner knitter...

Cast on an even number of stitches.
Row 1: [Knit 1, yarn over and slip the next stitch purlwise], repeat throughout the row. Turn.
Row 2: [Knit the yarn over and the slipped stitch together, yarn over and slip the next stitch purlwise], repeat throughout the row. Turn.
Repeat *row 2* for every row. That´s all!

Brioche Cape

"I made this Brioche cape when the cool weather of fall arrived. You just throw it over your shoulders, pin it together with a nice brooch or pin and become instantly warm - ahhhh.... It also looks really cool pinned over a coat or jacket. I borrowed my mother's first knitting needles, a whopping size 20 mm, for this project. She calls them her hippy needles because she used them to knit herself a sweater with big holes when she was a hippy back in the days. It's a lot of fun to knit with needles this big; I recommend everyone tries it!"

Erla wearing the cape

Size: width 38 cm/15 inches, length 120 cm/47 inches.
Yarn: Álafoss lopi, in light gray, 240 g (4 skeins). You can use any kind of yarn you want for this project, the weight doesn´t matter so much with the big needles!
Needles: 20 mm (US 36) circular needles.
Method: brioche stitch.

Cast on 18 stitches, or more if you like to have the cape wider than ca. 38 cm/15 inches. Just be sure to cast on an even number of stitches. Knit brioche stitch for about 120 cm/47 inches (see instructions above).

Erla Sigurlaug

The Cool Cowl

Guys with scarves and cowls are so cool! Here's a super cool guy cowl. Girls, surprise your man with this - and then borrow it when he's not using it.

Size: length about 55-57 cm/22 inches, width around 16 cm/6½ inches.
Needles: 9 mm/US 13 round needles or long needles. You can also knit the cowl with smaller needles if you just cast on more stitches. Just remember to cast on an even number of stitches.
Yarn: this one is knit with Alfa (a mixture of green and black) and black Mandarin Classic (cotton) together, but you can use any soft yarn you like. You need about 100g of Alfa and just a little bit of Mandarin Classic.
Method: brioche stitch, see instructions on the previous page - don´t panic, it's actually a really easy method after a few rows!

Cast on 14 stitches, loosely. Knit brioche stitch until the cowl measures about 52-53 cm/20½ inches, being careful not to stretch the cowl when measuring (the brioche stitch is quite stretchy.) Now knit a garter stitch border with buttonholes like this: *Row 1:* Knit. *Row 2:* Knit. *Row 3:* make the **buttonholes:** [Yarn over, knit 2 together]. Work the buttonhole row like this: Knit 3, make a buttonhole, knit 4, make a buttonhole, knit 4, make a buttonhole, knit 3. *Row 4 – 6:* Knit. *Row 7:* Cast off.

Fasten the buttons on, lengthwise, to the other end of the cowl (see photo).

Davíð with the cool cowl

Crocheted Beret

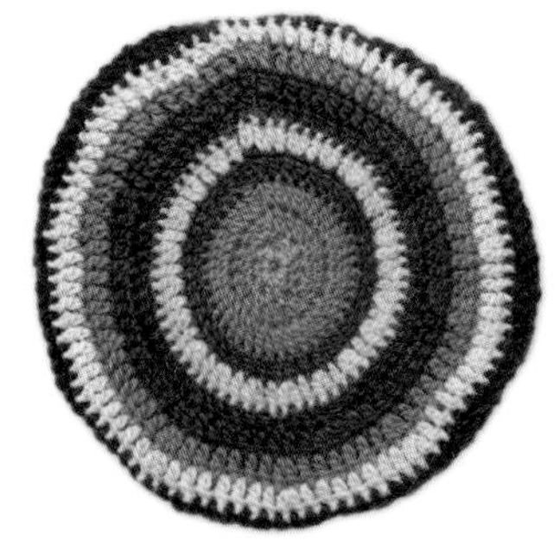

"Use your left over yarn for this hat and change the colors whenever you like! You can also make a more „plain" one in a single color. I have one that's hippy-like and multicolored to use when I am in that mood and also one that's more lady-like and simple for those kinds of days. What type of hat you get totally depends on the colors you choose. Make your own personal hat, it only takes one evening to make, and it also makes a brilliant personal gift."

Size: medium adult size. The hat is 28 cm/11 inches across.
Crochet hook: 6 mm (US J) but 5 mm (US H) also works well. With a 5 mm crochet hook you might have to work one extra round.
Yarn: Lopi lite – one or more colors, just as many as you like! 60 g for each hat. You can use other yarn of a similar weight that gives you the same gauge. Lopi lite is a worsted/light worsted yarn, and has approx. 100 m (109 yd)/50 g.
Gauge: 13 double crochets in 10 cm/4 inches.
Note: *this pattern uses American English crochet terminology, see page 29 for British crochet terms.*

This hat is worked in the round, using the double crochet (dc) stitch. All rounds end with a slip stitch in the first stitch of the round to join. Start by chaining 4, join with a slip stitch in first chain.
Round 1: chain 2 (counts as first dc) and then work 9 dc in the ring. *Round 2:* chain 2 (counts as first dc) work 2 dc in every st, the first dc into the same stitch the chain comes from. *Round 3:* chain 2, work 2 dc in each st around. *Round 4:* chain 2, work 1 dc in each st around. *Round 5:* chain 2, *dc in next st, 2 dc in the next st, repeat from *. *Round 6 and 7:* chain 2, dc in each st around. *Round 8:* chain 2, *dc in each of next 6 sts, 2 dc in next st, repeat from *. *Round 9:* chain 2 , *dc in each of next 7 sts, 2 dc in next st, repeat from *. *Round 10:* chain 2, *dc in each of next 6 sts, 2 dc in next st, repeat from *. *Round 11-12:* chain 2, work 1 dc in each st around. Now the hat is about 28 cm/11 inches across. If you want the hat to be bigger you work another round like round 11-12 before you start decreases. Now you start decreasing by working two stitches in to one dc; twin-dc**. *Round 13:* Work twin–dc** around. If you want to make the hat larger work more rounds like round 12 (1 dc in each st around) before you start the decreases. *Round 14-15:* chain 2, work 1 dc in each st around. If the hat is too wide it's easy to make it smaller by working single crochets in the last round and decreasing by skipping some sts. You can also weave elastic thread in the inside the edge of the hat to make it snug. If you feel the hat is not deep enough after these 15 rounds, work a few more rounds like round 15 (work 1 dc in each st around).

***Twin-dc: Two dc´s are joined into one to decrease like this: Start your first dc by making a yarn over, insert your hook in the next stitch and pull the yarn through. Make a yarn over and pull through the first 2 loops on your hook. Now you have 2 loops left on your hook, but instead of repeating this last step to finish your dc, move directly on to making another dc. Make a yarn over, insert your hook in the next stitch and pull the yarn through. Make a yarn over and pull through the first 2 stitches on your hook. Now finish the whole thing by making a yarn over and pulling through all the 3 loops on your hook. Now you have worked 2 stitches into 1 dc.*

Halldóra

Halldóra Skarphéðinsdóttir is a 41 year old Ph.D. in marine ecotoxicology and one of the authors of this book. She lives with her family and the other Svensons in Sweden. She comes from a long line of crafty and creative people, and she takes after her family in that respect. She started knitting when she was very young, and it's been a way for her to express herself creatively ever since – in between weighing amphipods in the lab where she is works. Halldóra is also one of the authors of the Icelandic knitting book Prjóniprjón (Knit-knit) that was published in 2008. After that, there was no question in her mind that she wanted to keep on knitting, designing and publishing knitting books. "How boring life must be for those who don´t knit..."

Knitting motto: *More knitting - more happiness*

Unnur Sóldís little elf

The Elf Hat

This hat is such a great project. Fast, easy, and makes your sweetheart super cute. This hat makes me smile every time I see it... :-)

Size: 6-12 months (1-2) 3+ years, or to fit a head size about 41 (46) 50 cm/16 (18) 19¾ inches in circumference. This hat can easily be made larger by adding 4, 8 or 12 stitches.
Yarn: Lucca merino wool, in orange (here, a Kool aid hand dyeing experiment) and Kambgarn, in red, 1 skein of each, or other yarn of similar weight that gives you the same gauge. Kambgarn has approx. 149 m (163 yd)/ 50 g.
Needles: 2.5 mm and 3.5 mm (US 1.5 and 4) 40 cm /16 inches circular needles and 3.5 mm (US 4) double pointed needles.
Gauge: 21 sts in stockinette stitch with 3,5 mm (US 4) should be 10 cm/4 inches. Change needle size to obtain the correct gauge, or increase/decrease the number of stitches you cast on to get a good fit. Just remember the number of stitches has to be divisible by 4.

Cast on 84 (96) 104 stitches with orange yarn and 2.5 mm (US 1.5) circular needles. Join to knit in the round and work 2x2 ribbing (knit 2, purl 2) for 8 rounds. Change to 3.5 mm (US 4) needles and knit stockinette stitch. Knit 5 rows with orange, and 2 rows with red throughout the hat. Knit until the hat measures 8 (9) 11 cm/3 (3 ½) 4½ inches. Now place 4 markers evenly spread throughout the row (after every 21. (24.) 26. stitches). **A.** [Knit to marker, knit 2 sts together], repeat until end of row (= 4 stitch decrease). **B.** Knit 3 rows. Repeat A and B untill only 8 stitches are left. Change to double pointed needles when the stitches become too few to fit on the circular needles. Break yarn and pull it through the remaining stitches. Weave in all loose ends. **Pom-pom:** I made a pom-pom by winding the yarn around a flat 6 cm/ 2½ inch wide frying stick (!). Tie the yarn around one end and sew the pom-pom together. Cut all threads at the other end, use a crochet needle to chain for 2-3 cm/1 inch and use it to fasten the pom-pom to the hat. Put the hat on some little cutie´s head and take a walk in the park, spreading sunshine all over...

The Ordinary Mittens

"I love these mittens because they're warm and cozy, simple, yet fun and quick to knit. This is the pattern I hunt around for every fall when the cold weather suddenly arrives: How many stitches do I cast on again? How many rounds do I knit up to the thumb? And so on. But look no further, here's my pattern for basic warm woolen mittens. The colors you use can of course be a little more natural than the ones shown here; these mittens would, for example, look nice in undyed wool. But why not make them a little bling-bling and happy? Let your inner colormonster run wild and mix unexpected colors together – works like magic to brighten your day during the dark winter months."

Size: medium, 27 cm/10½ inches long and 9 cm/3½ inches wide. You can get larger mittens (size L) by using 3 strands of the Icelandic unspun wool instead of 2, and 6 mm (US 10) needles instead of 5 mm (US 8).
Yarn: 2 strands Icelandic unspun wool, 60 g. The color pattern is great for using up leftover yarn, and you don't have to limit yourself to Icelandic unspun. You could also use Lopi lite or Lopi, and don't worry even though these yarns are of a different weight than the unspun, that just adds texture. Or you can use other yarn of similar weight that gives you the same gauge. The Icelandic unspun has approx. 300 m (328 yd)/100 g.
Needles: 4 and 5 mm (US 6 and 8) double pointed needles. Adjust needle size if necessary to obtain the correct gauge.
Gauge: 15 sts with 2 ply Icelandic unspun and 5 mm (US 8) needles in stockinette stitch should be 10 cm/4 inches.

Cast on 28 stitches with 4 mm (US 6) needles (cast on over 2 needles held together, so the cast on won't be too tight). Divide the stitches evenly between 4 needles and join to knit in the round, and knit 2x2 rib (knit 2, purl 2) for about 14 rows or 6 cm/2½ inches. Now switch to 5 mm (US 8) needles and knit stockinette stitch for 14 rows. On the next row make the opening for the thumb. **Left mitten:** Knit the 6 last stitches on needle 2 on to scrap yarn for the thumb opening. Move the 6 scrap yarn stitches back on to the left needle and knit them again with the main color. Knit to the end of the row. **Right mitten:** knit the first 6 stitches on needle 3 on to scrap yarn for the thumb opening, then move them back on to the left needle and knit them again with the main color. Knit to the end of the row. Knit 10 rows, then knit the color pattern according to the chart. After the pattern knit 7 rows with the main color, then begin decreasing for the top of the mitten. **Decrease row:** needle 1: slip 1, knit 1, pass the slipped stitch over the knit one (skp), knit to end of needle. Second needle: knit until 2 stitches are left on the needle, knit 2 together. Third needle: same as first needle. Fourth needle: same as second needle. Repeat these decreases every row until 8 stitches remain, two on each needle. Break yarn and pull through the remaining stitches. **Thumb:** remove the scrap yarn from the 6 stitches that form the thumb opening, and pick up stitches to knit the thumb: 6 above the opening, 6 below the opening, and 1-2 on each side of the opening. Divide the stitches evenly between 3 needles and work the thumb in the round. Knit 1 row, then decrease the number of stitches to 14 (if you have more than that) by knitting 2 together on the sides of the thumb, as needed. Knit 14 rows, then decrease for the top of the thumb like you decreased for the top of the mitten, by knitting a skp for a left leaning decrease, and knitting 2 together for a right leaning decrease. 4 sts are decreased like this per row for the next two rows, leaving 6 stitches. Break yarn and pull through the remaining 6 stitches. Weave in all ends, and knit the other mitten.

The pattern on these mittens is a traditional pattern often used as a part of the Icelandic Lopi wool sweaters.

Pattern:

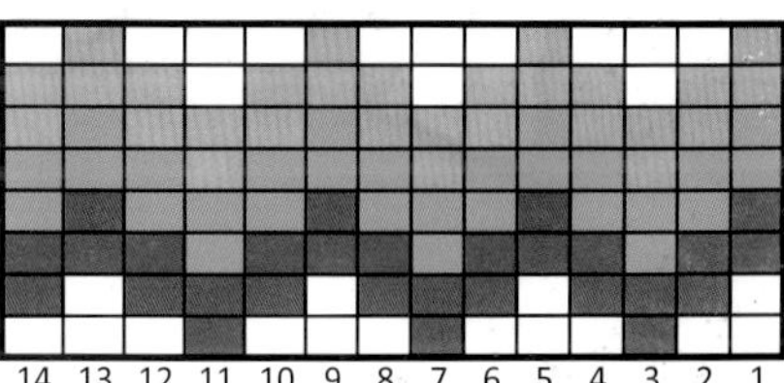

Halldóra

Lovely

A lovely A-shaped skirt knit from the waist down with simple lace at the bottom, made with the warmest of all wool: The Icelandic unspun. White like the snow, it turned out beautiful - I love it :-)

Size: small (medium) large, or to fit hips measuring 82 (92) 102 cm/32 (36) 40 inches. Total length of the skirt is about 44 (50) 56 cm/17 1/2 (20) 22 inches, but the length is easily adjustable.
Yarn: 200 (250) 300 g of unspun Icelandic wool, knit with 2 strands held together, or other yarn of similar weight that gives you the same gauge. The Icelandic unspun has approx. 300 m (328 yd)/100 g.
Needles: 5 mm (US 8) circular needles, 80 cm/32 inches. Adjust needle size if necessary to obtain the correct gauge.
Gauge: 12 sts in stockinette stitch should be 10 cm/4 inches.
Other: you will need an elastic band for the waist to hold the skirt up, and I also chose to line the skirt with fabric.

This skirt is knit from the waist down. Cast on 98 (110) 122 stitches with 2 strands of unspun Icelandic wool held together on 5 mm (US 8) circular needles. Join to work in the round and knit stockinette stitch for 10 cm/4 inches, then place 8 markers evenly spread throughout the next row; 1 on each side of the skirt, 3 evenly spread in the front and three in the back. Now increase 1 stitch on each side of the marker on each side of the skirt (= 4 sts are increased). Repeat these side increases every fourth row, three more times. In the same row that you make the last of these increases, also increase 1 stitch where each of the other markers is placed; 3 in front, and 3 in the back of the skirt (a total of 10 sts are increased in this row). **A.** Knit 4 cm/1½ inches. **B.** Knit an increase row: increase 1 stitch by each of the markers (a total of 8 stitches are increased). Repeat A and B three more times which gives a total of 152 (164) 176 stitches. Knit untill the skirt is 35 (40) 45 cm/14 (16) 18 inches long - or for as long as you want the stocki¬nette stitch part to be. Next round: increase 32 (43) 54 stitches evenly spread throughout the row, or just about in every 5 (4) 3rd stitch wich gives you a total of 184 (207) 230 stitches. The total number of stitches has to be divisible by 23 when starting the lace pattern below. Now, knit the lace pattern on the chart below for 9 (10) 11 cm/3½ (4) 4½ inches, or as long as you want the skirt to be (try it on!). Cast off and weave in all ends. Block the skirt - this is important with the Icelandic unspun, as it works like magic to smooth the bumps out. An elastic band that fits your waist (hips or where you want to place the skirt) is sewn into the waist of the skirt with a sewing machine. I choose to line my skirt with a thin stretchy fabric. Lay the skirt down on the floor and cut the lining fabric after the skirt, sew its sides together, and sew it,along with the elastic band, into the waist of the skirt.
Voila, the skirt is ready! Put it on and do a little dance :)

Hrefna in Lovely

Lace pattern at the bottom of skirt: *two rows that are repeated untill lace measures 10 cm/4 inches, or for as long as you please.*

o		o		o		o	/	/	/	/	\	\	\	\	o		o		o		o	

☐ Knit stitch

o Yarn over

/ K2tog. Knit two stitches together as one stitch (left stitch ends up on top)

\ Ssk. Slip 1 knitwise, Slip 1 knitwise, insert left hand needle into front of these two stitches and knit them together (rigth stitch ends up on top of the left one).

Emil

"I call this sweater Emil, because it reminds me of Emil (and his shirts), a famous character from novels by the Swedish author Astrid Lindgren. The sweater is knit in the round up to the sleeves, then the front and back pieces are knit separately, back and forth. This is a simple sweater, but the neckline detail adds interest to the knitting and character to the sweater."

Size: 1-2 (3-4) 5-6 years. The chest circumference under the arms is 70 (76) 82 cm/27½ (30) 32¼ inches. The length of the sweater is 38 (44) 50 cm/15 (17) 20 inches, and sleeve lenght under the arms is 24 (28) 31 cm/9½ (11) 12¼ inches.
Yarn: Einband, Icelandic laceweight; 100 (100) 150 g or other yarn of similar weight that gives you the same gauge. Einband, the Icelandic laceweight has approximately 229 m (250 yd)/50 g.
Needles: 4.5 mm (US 7) circular needles 60 cm/24 inches, and 3.5 and 4.5 mm (US 4 and 7) double pointed needles. Adjust needle size if necessary to obtain the correct gauge.
Gauge: 20 sts and 31 rows in stockinette stitch with 4.5 mm (US 7) needles should be 10x10 cm/4x4 inches.

Cast on 140 (152) 164 stitches with 4.5 mm (US 7) circular needles. Join to work in the round and alternate 1 knit row and 1 purled row for 8 rows to get a small garter stitch border. After that, knit stockinette stitch, untill the body measures 22 (26) 30 cm/8¾ (10¼) 12 inches. Now divide the body into a front and a back piece, with an equal amount of stitches in each part. Leave the back stitches on scrap yarn, stitch holder or spare circular needle and work only with the front piece. Knit on the right side, and purl on the wrong side until the front piece measures a total of 26 (30) 34 cm/10¼ (12) 13½ inches. Now it's time to make the opening in the front of the sweater. Find the exact middle of the front piece, and knit the middle 8 stitches in garter stitch (knit on both right and wrong side over these 8 stitches), for a total of 6 rows. Knit to the exact middle of the piece (with 4 garter sts on each side), and turn. Now work only with one side of the front and set the other one aside. Continue to knit, keeping the four stitches on the centre-facing edge in garter stitch and the rest of the stitches in stockinette stitch. When the front opening measures 6 (7) 8 cm/2½ (3) 3¼ inches, start making the neckline. **Neckline:** put the 4 garter stitch stitches on the edge on to scrap yarn (until the neckline edge is knitted in the end). Cast off 3 sts in the beginning of next two knit rows from the edge, then cast off 2 (3) 3 sts in the next knit row, and 1 st in the beginning of the next 5 (6) 8 rows from the edge. Knit until the front piece measures 38 (44) 50 cm/15 (17½) 19¾ inches, then cast off. Knit the other front side in the same manner. **Back:** continue with the back piece, knit on the right side and purl on the wrong side until the piece measures 35 (41) 47 cm/14 (16¼) 18½ inches. Then cast off for the neckline 18 (22) 26 sts exactly in the middle of the back piece. Now knit each shoulder separately. Cast off 3 sts on the edge of the neckline in the beginning of the next 3 rows from the neckline. Knit until the piece measures 38 (44) 50 cm/15 (17½) 20 inches, then cast off. Knit the other shoulder in the same manner. **Sleeves:** cast on 40 (44) 48 sts with 3.5 mm (US 4) double pointed needles and join to knit in the round. Knit garter stitch for 14 rows (knit 1 row, purl 1 row to get garter stitch since you are knitting in the round). Now, change to 4.5 mm (US 7) needles, place a marker at the beginning of the row and knit all rows. Increase 1 stitch on each side of the marker every 5th row untill the sleeve is sufficiently wide to fit in the sleeve opening, or about 16 (18) 20 cm/6¼ (7¼) 8 inches in diameter, then bind off. Knit the other sleeve. Sew the shoulders together, sew the sleeves on to the body and weave in all ends. **Neckline:** pick up stitches around the neckline on 3.5 mm (US 4) needles, also the 4 garter stitch stitches on each neckline edge that were left on a scrap yarn, and knit *moss/seed stitch** back and forth for 6-8 rows. Cast off loosely. Crochet with single crochet (sc) along the edge of the opening in the front of the sweater.

**Seed/moss stitch: knit 1, purl 1, and on the next row do the opposite: purl 1 on top of a knit stitch, knit 1 on top of a purl stitch.*

Halldóra

Purple Dream

- mittens that are both crocheted and knit

"These mittens are inspired by beautiful mittens from the North of Iceland, and I also use the assembly technique from Emelía's TV mittens earlier in the book."

Size: medium.
Yarn: Lopi lite or other yarn of similar weight, in two purple colors, and dark blue, white and grey-beige, 1 skein of each. Lopi lite is a worsted/light worsted yarn and has approx. 100 m (109 yd)/50 g.
Needles and hook: 5 mm (US 8) circular needles (double pointed needles are almost too short here), and a crochet hook nr. 5 -6 (US H-J). Every crocheted square should measure about 7-8 cm/2¾ - 3¼ inches on each side; use a crochet hook that will give you squares with these measurements.
Gauge: 14.5 sts in garter stitch on 5 mm (US 8) needles should be 10 cm/4 inches.
Note: *this pattern uses American English crochet terminology, see page 29 for British crochet terms.*

Begin with crocheting 3 squares for the back of the hand. These are then sewn together, and a border crocheted around them. Then stitches are picked up along one of the longer side of the piece, and garter stitch knit for the palm of the hand.

Crocheted square: chain 3 with purple yarn and a 5-6 mm (US H-J) crochet hook, join in to a circle with a slip stitch (st) in first chain. *Round 1:* chain 3 that counts as the first double crochet (dc), work 2 dc in the ring. [Chain 2 (will become the corner of the square), work 3 dc in the ring], repeat twice more, chain 2, join with a slip stitch to the first dc. Break yarn. *Round 2:* with another color, join in one of the four corners and chain 3 that counts as the first dc. [Work dc in each of the dc in the first row = 3 dc, then 2 dc in the corner, chain 2, 2 dc in the same corner], repeat for all four sides of the square, all sides of the square should now have 7 dc. Join with a slip stitch in the first dc. *Round 3:* change to grey-beige and work cingle crochet (sc) around the square, 1 in each dc and 4 in each corner, a total of 11 sc on each side. Break yarn. Crochet 2 more squares like this, but change the order of the colors you use. When all three squares are ready, sew them together into one long piece. Now work sc with dark blue around the piece, except for on one of the short sides, where the cuff will be placed. Start in the corner of one of the long sides and make a total of 77 sc around three sides of the piece. Break yarn, work another round of sc with white, and then another with purple. Now pick up 33 stitches with 5 mm (US 8) circular needles along one of the long sides of the piece to start knitting the palm of the hand. The palm is knit in garter stitch, so every row is knit. Start knitting at the edge where the cuff will be. When one stitch is left on the needle, pick up the nearest sc stitch on the short side of the piece and knit it together with the last stitch on the needle. This is done to close the mitten's top. This is, however, not done for the first and the last ridge (since there are more garter stitch rows than single crochet sts to pick up where the top of the fingers will be). **Left mitten:** knit 2 rows, then make the opening for the thumb: Knit 15 sts, turn. Leave the 18 sts on a stitch holder and knit the 15 sts back and forth for 10 rows (creating 5 ridges) from the beginning of the thumb opening. Then knit the 18 sts (leaving the 15 sts waiting on a stitch holder) for 10 rows (creating 5 ridges). Now continue knitting all 33 sts of the piece, knitting also over the stitches placed on a holder onto the needle. Knit 16 more rows, a total of 28 knitted rows.
Right mitten: using the same method as for the other mitten but mirroring the opening´s placement in the palm. Knit 16 rows, then make the opening for the thumb, knit 15 sts, turn. Leave the 18 sts on a stitch holder and knit the 15 sts back and forth for 10 rows, then knit the 18 sts back and forth for 10 rows as well. Knit the 15 stitches left on a holder onto the needle and knit over all sts a total of 2 rows after the thumb opening. Now it's time to cast off, which is done by knitting the palm piece together with the other side of the crocheted piece to save you from sewing it together in the end. Pick up 33 stitches on a needle along the other long side of the

crocheted piece. With the wrong side of the mitten facing out, knit 2 sts together, 1 from each needle, (1 crocheted stitch, and 1 knit stitch), onto a third needle. Knit 2 sts like that together again and bind off by passing the first stitch over the second. Repeat this until one stitch remains on your right needle. Break the yarn and pull it through the stitch. This method of binding off is usually referred to as the three needle bind off. **Thumb:** pick up 14 sts around the thumb opening, about 5 above it, 5 in below it, and 2 on each side. Join to knit in the round and knit garter stitch (knit 1 row, purl 1 row). Knit 8 ridges (16 rounds), then, on the next row, knit 2 stitches together throughout the row. Break the yarn and pull through the remaining stitches. **Crochet a picot edge** on the opening of the mitten with white yarn: Work 1 single crochet in the space between the ridges in the palm, chain 4, join with a slip stitch in fourth chain from hook, work 1 sc in the next space between ridges, and repeat this around the opening of the mitten. When crocheting over the back of the hand, work 1 single crochet into every other stitch.

The Earflap Hat

"This is my favorite hat to make for the little ones. The earflaps keep the ears warm, and it can be tied under the chin, so little hands can't remove it – not without a bit of a struggle at least. And it's very cute as well."

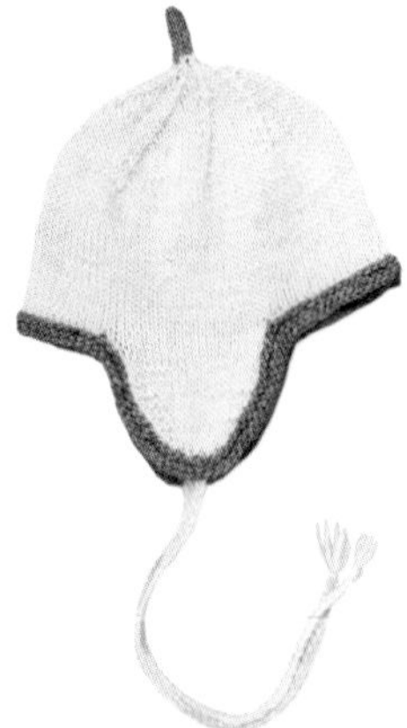

Size: 1 (2) 3 years.
Yarn: Eco baby wool from Marks & Kattens, or Kambgarn or other yarn of the same weight that gives you same gauge. Kambgarn is a sportweight yarn and has approx. 149 m (163 yd)/ 50 g.
Needles: 3.5 mm (US 4) double pointed and circular needles, 40 cm/16 inches. Adjust needle size if necessary to obtain the correct gauge.
Gauge: 22 stitches in stockinette stitch should be 10 cm /4 inches.

Start by knitting the earflaps. Knit one at a time, back and forth, knit on the right side, purl on the wrong side (stockinette stitch). Cast on 10 stitches, knit 1 row. Then increase by 1 stitch at the beginning of each row until you have 20 stitches. Knit stockinette stitch without increasing until the earflap is 6 cm/2¼ inches long. Set aside and knit the other earflap. When the other earflap is ready, with the right side facing, cast on 36 (41) 46 stitches for the front piece of the hat, using the working yarn from the second earflap. You need to switch to circular needles now. Knit the first earflap on to the hat with the right side facing. Using the working yarn, cast on 20 (23) 26 stitches for the back of the hat. You should have a total of 96 (104) 112 stitches. Join to knit in the round and knit 8 (9) 10 cm/3¼ (3½) 4 inches, then begin decreasing for the top of the head. **Decreases:** [knit 10 (11) 12 stitches, knit 2 together], repeat throughout the row. Knit 1 row. [Knit 9 (10) 11 stitches, knit 2 together], repeat throughout the row. Knit 1 row. Continue like this with a decreasing number of stitches between the decreases until only 8 stitches are left. Change to double pointed needles when the stitches have become too few to fit on the circular needles. Now change to brown yarn, and knit 8 rows with the 8 stitches that are left. Knit 2 and 2 stitches together, break the yarn and pull it through the remaining 4 stitches. **Finishing:** you can work single crochet around the edges of the hat with brown yarn, or pick up stitches and knit a border. To knit a border, pick up 1 stitch in every stitch in the front and the back of the hat, and around each earflap it should be sufficient to pick up 42 stitches. Knit garter stitch back and forth for 4 rows, cast off. Sew the edges of the border together with a few stitches. Weave in all ends. The ties can either be made by knitting an I-cord, or made by braids: 3 strands of yarn in each of the 3 strands that you braid together to make a tie. Each tie is 25 cm/10 inches long. Sew the ties to the earflaps.

Halldóra

Möbius

A Möbius strip is an interesting mathematical phenomenon. It's a strip that has only one side and one edge. It is named after the German mathematician August Ferdinand Möbius who first described it in the year 1858. A knitted Möbius is a beautiful shawl that lies over the shoulders with one half twist in the front. When it's knit, it grows in two directions at once since with every row you add length both above and below the middle of the shawl. It's very important to have a long circular needle for this project (80 cm/32 inches is an absolute minimum), because the möbius is knit with the needles coiled up in a circle. It's also very important to get the cast on right, but after that you just keep on knitting round and round...

How to cast on for a Möbius

It's vital to get the cast on right when knitting a Möbius, so that you only get one half twist in the shawl. Here we walk you through how to do it with both photos and text. This method of casting on is attributed to Cat Bordhi, who's posted an excellent YouTube video that shows you how to cast on for a Möbius.

1. Start by making a slip-knot and put it on your circular needles, letting them coil like shown in the photo. **2.** Using the right needle, go under the cable and retreive the yarn (like the cable is a huge stitch that you are knitting in). Now you have the first stitch on your right needle. **3.** Make a yarn over, this is the second stitch. **4.** Repeat 2 and 3 until you have the number of stitches you need for your project. With this method, stitches are formed both on the needle and its cable. But you should only count the stitches on the needle itself. In this photo 4 stitches have been cast on. **5.** When you have cast on the number of stitches needed, you should check that there's only one half twist on the needles. The needle and cable should lie parallel to each other all around the circle, but one end of the needle should cross the cable only once (as you can see in the red circle in the photo if you study it closely (with a magnifying glass!)) This is very important, since a Möbius has only one half twist. Now you can start knitting the stitches on the left needle. The first stitch is the slip-knot you made in the beginning. Place a marker to mark the beginning of the round. **6.** Now knit the stitches on the left needle. Before you know it, you have begun to knit the "lower" stitches of the cast on. When knitting a Möbius you knit 1 round above the middle, and 1 round below the middle, so the piece grows outward from the middle.

1.

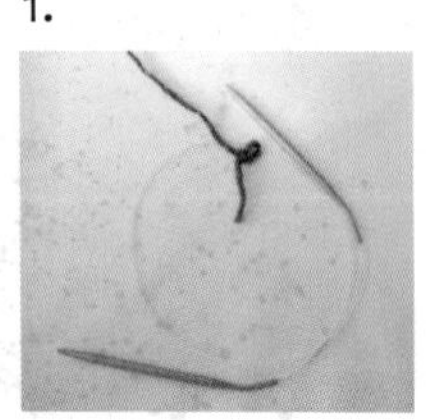

2.

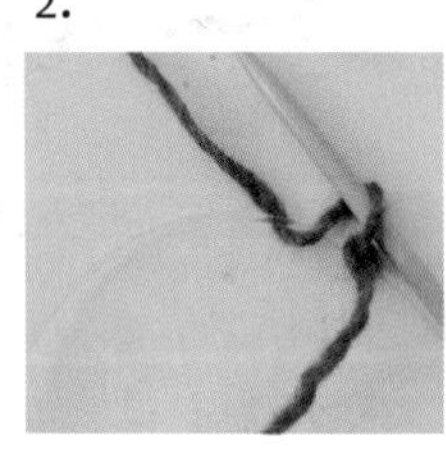

3.

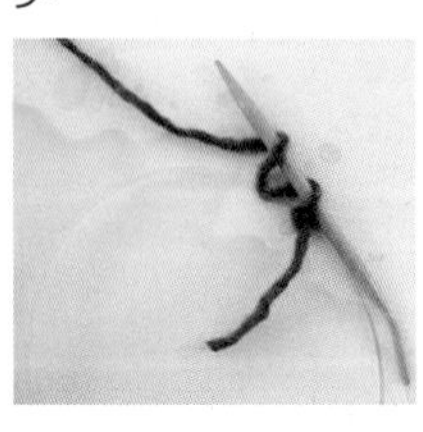

4.

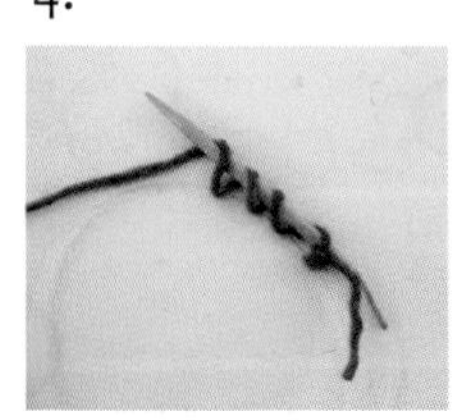

5.

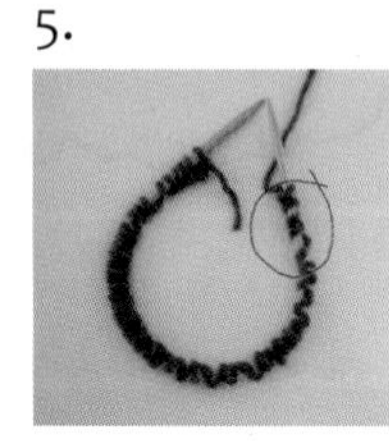

6.

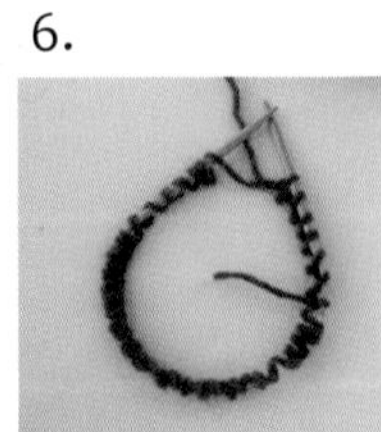

Hrefna Björk Birgisdóttir

To knit a Möbius Shawl

Size: smaller (larger), or about 100 (120) cm/40 (47) inches in circumference. The purple and pink Möbius is 100 cm/40 inches. It's a good idea to wrap a tape measure around your shoulders to get an idea of what size of a shawl would fit you.
Yarn: Einband, Icelandic laceweight wool or another laceweight yarn that gives you the same gauge, in two colors, 1 skein of each. The Icelandic laceweight has approx. 229 m (250 yd)/50 g.
Needles: 6 mm (US 10) circular needles. 80 cm/32 inches long is absolute mininum – the needles should preferably be longer.
Gauge: 10 stitches in garter stitch should be 10 cm/4 inches.

Cast on 100 (120) stitches like described on the previous page and join to work in the round. Place a stitch marker at the beginning of the row. Alternate a knit row with a purl row to work the piece in garter stitch. Change colors as you like and work a total of 50 ridges (counted over the whole piece), or until piece is approximately 50 cm/ 20 inches long. Cast off loosely. Knit a decorative eyelet pattern in the shawl like this: [knit 2 together, yarn over], repeat throughout the row. The pink and purple shawl is knit like this: 24 rows with pink (that is in the middle, the shawl grows from the middle), change to purple and knit an eyelet row. Knit 10 rows, knit another eyelet row, knit 4 rows, change to pink, knit 3 rows. Knit 1 row with purple, 2 with pink, work an eyelet row, now 6 rows with pink, work an eyelet row, knit 1 and 1 row alternatively with purple and pink for 6 rows, then 6 rows with purple, cast off. Alternating colors every row produces a smoother color transition and gives the shawl a nice look.

Perla

Google "Möbius cast on" and watch Cat Bordhi's instructional video about how to cast on for a Möbius.

Halldóra

The Sideways Knit Cardigan

"This is such a fun pattern. This cardigan is knit sideways in one piece, sleeves and everything. When the knitting is done you only need to sew the sleeves together under the arms. I first saw a similar pattern in a Swedish book of doll clothing patterns that had been copied from old baby clothes. This is an old pattern, at least from the 1940s (but the old stuff is often the best stuff). Here the pattern is adjusted for knitting with the sportweight Kambgarn."

Size: 6-12 months (12-18months) 2 years (3-4 years).
Yarn: Kambgarn in green, lime orange and white, 1 skein of each, or other sportweight yarn that gives you the same gauge. Kambgarn has approximately 149 m (163 yd)/ 50 g.
Needles: 3.5 mm (US 4) circular needles (the length doesn't matter, the sweater is knit back and forth). Adjust needle size if necessary to obtain the correct gauge.
Gauge: 20 stitches in garter stitch = 10 cm/4 inches.

This sweater is knit in garter stitch with every fourth ridge knit in white yarn. Start by knitting the **left front:** loosely, cast on 60 (66) 74 (80) stitches with orange yarn, do not join. Knit 12 rows back and forth in garter stitch; this is the buttonband. Then work the following six rows that are repeated throughout the whole sweater:

1. With right side facing, change to white yarn and knit until 6 stitches are left on the left needle, turn the piece* and knit back = 2 rows white garter stitch up to the neckline (the last 6 stitches) of the cardigan.
2. Change to your main color. Knit all stitches and back = 2 rows garter stitch over the whole piece.
3. Knit with the main color until 20 (22) 24 (26) stitches remain on the left needle, then turn* and knit back = 2 rows garter stitch up to the yoke.
Repeat these six rows until the piece measures 18 (19) 20 (22) cm/7 (7½) 8 (8¾) inches, then it's time to start knitting the first sleeve. **First Sleeve:** place the first 36 (40) 46 (50) stitches counting from the lower edge of the sweater, on a stitch holder or some scrap yarn, but continue to work with the upper part (yoke) of the sweater. Continuing on from the yoke, cast on 32 (35) 46 (53) stitches for the sleeve, for example with the backward loop method. The sleeve is knit along with the shoulder in one piece, with the 6 row pattern repeat as before – with one exception: the first 4 stitches on the lower edge of the sleeve are only knit with the main color; the white stripe is only knit from the 5th stitch onward. This is done to narrow the sleeve a bit at the cuff. Knit the sleeve until it measures 17 (18) 18 (20) cm/ 6¾ (7) 7 (8) inches (measured where widest), then cast off the extra 32 (35) 46 (53) sleeve stitches. Now pick up the stitches that waited on a holder while you knit the sleeve and join them with the yoke again. **Back:** knit the 6 row pattern until the back measures 31 (35) 37 (40) cm/12¼ (13¾) 14½ (15¾) inches, then place the first 36

(40) 46 (50) stitches from the lower edge of the sweater on to a stitch holder or some scrap yarn. In this cardigan I switched to lime green in the middle of the back (see photo), and to dark green when I began the second sleeve. **Second sleeve:** cast on for the second sleeve and knit it like the first one. **Right front:** when the second sleeve is finished and the sleeve stitches have been bound off, knit the stitches that were left waiting on a help needle or a thread together with the yoke stitches; you are now knitting the right front piece. Knit until the front piece measures 16 (17) 18 (20) cm/6¼ (6¾) 7 (8) inches. Now break the white yarn, and make the front band. With main color, knit garter stitch over the whole piece back and forth (no short rows) for 6 rows, then make the buttonholes on the upper part of the cardigan. The buttonholes are made like this: [knit 2 together, yarn over]. The top buttonhole should be placed 4 stitches from the top, and the other ones below that with 6-8 cm/2½ - 3 inches between. Knit 7 more rows, and bind off loosely. **Finishing:** sew the sleeves together under the arms. Sew on buttons, weave in all loose ends.

**When knitting short rows, i.e. turning to knit back without finishing the row, small holes are formed. To prevent the holes you can wrap the yarn around the first stitch on the right needle (after you've turned and are about to knit back). Actually, the holes can be quite decorative and look like an eyelet row directly under the yoke (the last two rows of the pattern repeat, see no. 3). It´s simply a matter of taste if you want to have holes on your sweater or not.*

Flower Hat

Sizes: 6 – 12 months (1-2 years) 2-3 years, or a hat with a circumference of 41 (45) 49 cm/ 16 (17½) 19½ inches.
Yarn: Lucca merino wool, in green and white, or Kambgarn or other yarn of similar weight that gives you same gauge. For the crocheted flower, use leftovers of yarn with similar weight; green for the stem, and pink for the flower.
Needles and hook: 3 and 4 mm (US 3 and 6) double pointed and circular needles, 40 cm/16 inches long for the hat itself. 3 mm crochet hook (US D) for the flower.
Gauge: 20 stitches in stockinette stitch with needles 4 should be 10 cm/4 inches.

Cast on 81 (90) 99 stitches, with green yarn on 3 mm (US 3) circular needles. Join to knit in the round and knit rib (knit 1, purl 1) for 4 rows. This hat is knit with 1 white row in every 8th row. After the ribbing, change to 4 mm (US 6) needles and knit stockinette stitch for 11 (12) 14 cm/4½ (4¾) 5½ inches, then it's time to decrease for the top of the head.
Decreases: [Knit 7 stitches, knit 2 together] until end of row. Knit 1 row. [Knit 6 stitches, knit 2 together] until end of row. Knit 1 row. Continue like this with a decreasing number of stitches between the decreases until only 5 stitches are left. Cut the yarn and pull through the remaining stitches. Weave in all ends.

Flower: the flower is crocheted. **Note:** *this pattern uses American crochet terminology, see page 29 for British crochet terms.* With pink yarn and a 3 mm (US D) crochet needle: chain 2. *Round 1:* work 5 single crochet in second chain from hook. *Round 2:* crochet a flower petal in each stitch: 1 single crochet, 1 half double crochet, 2 double crochet, 1 half double crochet, 1 single crochet. Make flower petals like this in the other 4 sts that are left. Cut yarn. *Stem:* With green yarn and 3 mm (US D) crochet hook, chain 20 + 3 for the first double crochet. Now work 3 double crochet in each of the 20 chains. Sew the flower to the stem, and the stem to the top of the hat, weave in ends. Done!

Halldóra

Rosie the Red

Unnur Sóldís wearing Rosie the Red

This hat is so sweet and simple. The stitch pattern is very simple and consists of just 3 rows that are repeated throughout the hat. Easy to memorize (- and easy to forget actually...). The pattern is not a real cable pattern, but it does look like tiny cables.

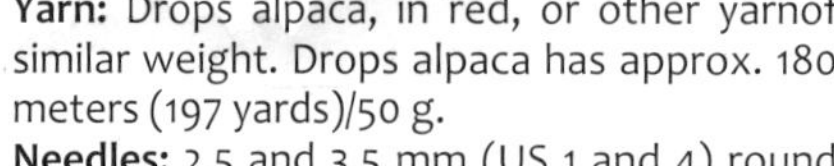

Size: small – or from 1 year (medium) large. Or a hat that fits a head 47 (49) 52+ cm/18½ (19½) 20½ inches in circumference. The pattern is very stretchy. The depth of the hat is adjustable to your taste, some prefer it to be slouchy, but here the pattern is of average depth and "non-slouchy".

Yarn: Drops alpaca, in red, or other yarnof similar weight. Drops alpaca has approx. 180 meters (197 yards)/50 g.
Needles: 2.5 and 3.5 mm (US 1 and 4) round needles 40 cm/16 inches long and 3.5 mm (US 4) double pointed needles.
Gauge: 21 stitches in stockinette stitch with needles 3,5 mm (US 4) should be 10 cm/4 inches.

Cast on 104 (108) 112 stitches on 2.5 mm (US 1) circular needles, and knit 2x2 ribbing (knit 2, purl 2) for 4 (5) 6 cm/1½ (2) 2½inches. Then increase 1 purl stitch in every 4th (purled) stitch over the next round. Change to 3.5 mm (US 4) circular needles and knit the **"tiny-cable" pattern:**
Row 1: [purl 3 sts, knit 1, yarn over, knit 1], repeat to the end of the row.
Row 2: [purl 3 sts, knit 3 sts], repeat to the end of the row.
Row 3: [purl 3 sts, slip 1 st knitwise, knit 1 stitch, knit another stitch, pass the slipped stitch over the two knitted stitches], repeat to the end of the row.
Knit this pattern until the hat measures 13 (15) 18 cm/5¼ (6) 7¼ inches – or more if you want it to be slouchy, then begin decreasing for the top of the head. **Decreases:** purl 2 of the purled stitches together throughout the row, so now only 2 instead of 3 purled stitches are between the tiny faux cables. Knit 4 (6) 8 more rows. Purl 2 purled stitches together, and knit 2 of the knitted stitches together through the row (after row 3 in the tiny cable pattern). Now you have 1 knit and 1 purled stitch alternating through the row. Knit 1, purl 1, for the next 3 rows, then knit 2 and 2 sts together. Knit 1 row, and then knit 2 stitches together for 1 row. Cut the yarn, pull through the remaining stitches and weave in the ends. Rosie is ready!